Canadian Biography Series

LEONARD COHEN: A LIFE IN ART

*Cohen performing in Mainz,
Germany, on 4 May 1988.*

Leonard Cohen

A LIFE IN ART

Ira Nadel

ECW PRESS

CANADIAN CATALOGUING IN PUBLICATION DATA

Nadel, Ira Bruce
Leonard Cohen : a life in art
Includes bibliographical references.
ISBN 1-55022-210-4

1. Cohen, Leonard, 1934– – Biography. 2. Poets, Canadian
(English) – 20th century – Biography.* 1. Title.

PS8505.072Z73 1994   C811'.54   C94-930594-4
PR9199.3.C65Z73 1994

This book has been published with the assistance of the Ministry
of Culture, Recreation and Tourism of the Province of Ontario,
through funds provided by the Ontario Publishing Centre, and with
the assistance of grants from the Department of Communications,
The Canada Council, the Ontario Arts Council, and the Government
of Canada through the Canadian Studies and Special Projects
Directorate of the Department of the Secretary of State of Canada.

Design and imaging by ECW Type & Art, Oakville, Ontario.
Printed by Imprimerie Gagné, Louiseville, Québec.

Distributed by General Distribution Services,
30 Lesmill Road, Toronto, Ontario M3B 2T6,
(416) 445-3333, (800) 387-0172 (Canada), FAX (416) 445-5967.

Distributed to the trade in the United States exclusively
by InBook, 140 Commerce Street, P.O. Box 120261,
East Haven, Connecticut, U.S.A. 06512,
(203) 467-4257, FAX (203) 469-8364.
Customer service: (800) 243-0138, FAX (800) 334-3892.

Distributed in the United Kingdom by Drake Marketing,
St. Fagans Road, Fairwater, Cardiff CF5 3AE (0222) 560333.

Published by ECW PRESS,
2120 Queen Street East,
Toronto, Ontario M4E 1E2.

ACKNOWLEDGEMENTS

In Montreal: Louis Dudek, Hazel Field, Morton Rosengarten, Bruce White-man, Rhona and Michael Kenneally, Joseph and Joanne Ronsley for collective help and generosity; in Ottawa: Brian Turner at the National Archives for assistance; in Toronto: Doug and Janet Fetherling for encouragement, Daniel Richler for the chance to discuss Leonard Cohen on TV Ontario's *Imprint*, the staff at the Thomas Fisher Rare Book Library for direction, David Mayerovitch for new light on past summers; in Vancouver: my children, Dara and Ryan, for their love and curiosity, Pamela Dalziel for listening, Charles Bolding for research, Alan Twigg for the records, James McClaren for the tapes, Michael Pacey for sources, Thomas Friedman for new directions; in Victoria: Stephen Scobie for details; in New York: Robert Bower for his support; in Europe: Yvonne Hakze and Bea de Koning for information; in San Diego: my mother, Frances Sofman Nadel, for her careful reading; in San Francisco: Soheyl Dahi for his friendship; in Los Angeles: Kelly Lynch, Joan Lynch, and Sarah Rich for assistance; and everywhere: Leonard Cohen.

PHOTOGRAPHS: Cover photo, 1992, R. Galbraith, © Canapress Photo Service, is used by permission of Canapress Photo Service; frontispiece illustration, 1988, © Sven Zippmann, is used by permission of the photographer; illustration 2, in Jacques Vassal, *Leonard Cohen* (Paris: Albin Michel, 1974); illustration 3, 1955, *Old McGill*, is used by permission of McGill University; illustration 4, © Leonard Cohen, is used by permission of Leonard Cohen; illustration 5, 1963, Allan R. Leishman, *Montreal Star*, is used by permission of the National Archives of Canada PA 190165; illustration 6, 1964, © *Gazette* [Montreal], is used by permis-sion of the *Gazette*; illustration 7, 1966, © John Max; illustration 8, 1967, © Bob Cato, CBS Records/Sony Music Entertainment (Canada) Inc.; illustration 9, 1968, © Roz Kelly; illustration 10, 1969, C.P. Noyes, © McClelland and Stewart, is used by permission of McClelland and Stewart; illustration 11, 1970, Jean-Pierre Leloir, in Jacques Vassal, *Leonard Cohen* (Paris: Albin Michel, 1974); illustration 12, 1970, Pierre Brosseau, *Montreal Star*, is used by permission of the National Archives of Canada PA 190159; illustration 13, 1973, © S. Elrod, CBS Records/Sony Music Entertainment (Canada) Inc.; illustration 14, 1975, © Gino, CBS Records/Sony Music Entertainment (Canada) Inc.; illustration 15, 1983, © Dominique Issermann, is used by permission of the photographer; illustration 16, 1984, © *Gazette* [Montreal], is used by permission of the *Gazette*; illustration 17, 1985, © Dominique Issermann, is used by permission of the photographer; illustration 18, 1988, © Christof Graf, is used by permission of the photogra-pher; illustration 19, 1988, © Christof Graf, is used by permission of the

To keep our inward conscience clear and to
know whether we can take responsibility for
our creative experiences just as they stand
in all their truthfulness and absoluteness:
that is the basis of every work of art. . . .

— Rainer Maria Rilke

TABLE OF CONTENTS

LIST OF ILLUSTRATIONS

Leonard Cohen

A LIFE IN ART

"MY LIFE IN ART"

Early morning in a sunlit suite on the fifth floor of a Hollywood hotel. A woman whose beauty rivals Lady Hamilton's lies asleep on the bed. Next to her is a man visibly distracted, staring at the clock and out the window. His desires fulfilled, he declares the moment "the end of my life in art" (Cohen, *Death of a Lady's Man* 190). Slowly, he explains why: his encounter with "the full measure of beauty" has been so great that it has exhausted his creativity (190). At last, in his forty-first year, he knows love — but also betrayal, for his command of art suddenly weakens in the face of intolerable pleasure. Peace, when it comes, occurs only through sexual bliss, which substitutes intensity for anxiety. The double irony of the setting of Leonard Cohen's manifesto "My Life in Art" is that sex brings death not life, paralysis not energy: "Six-fifty [a.m.]. Ruined in Los Angeles. . . . I want to die in her arms and leave her" (192). Doubting his courage, the narrator ends the passage pleading for an alter ego to tell him "about the noble ones who conquered all of this" (192).

Leonard Cohen at the Château Marmont on Sunset Boulevard in the summer of 1974 is, at first glance, an unlikely place to begin an account of his life in art. Yet the scene depicts a representative moment, if not posture, for Cohen, who, when entrapped by beauty, finds his art imperilled. He responds by seeking freedom, recognizing the need to dismantle love so that he can sustain "the poignant immortality of my life in art" (*Death of a Lady's Man* 191) — for only art can truly seduce Leonard Cohen. He has repeatedly moved from ruin to resurrection in his nearly forty-year career, often duplicating this situation where the attainment of an engulfing love inhibits his art. His only response has been rejection. Yet the pain of such rejection becomes the very material of his art: witness the tortuous poems of loss in *The Energy of Slaves* or songs such as "Take This Longing" and "Ain't No Cure for Love." But Cohen's dismissal of women makes him more appealing; hence, when he sings about the loss of love, he becomes loved all the more. Nevertheless, he confesses that many lives have been overthrown for what he calls, in "Days of Kindness," the final poem of *Stranger Music*, "an education in the world" (401).

From a youthful interest in country-and-western music to a mature interest in computer graphics, Cohen has been absorbed by the effort to render desire through art. His poetry, fiction, and lyrics all record this obsession, which has variously taken on lyrical, aggressive, or spiritual tones. But the need to create is foremost, the driving dimension of his life in reaction to the middle-class world of Westmount, the isolation but creative freedom of Hydra, and the stimulation of the musical world in New York and Los Angeles. Art, in any of its many expressions, provides for Cohen the means to confront and master his desires, weaknesses, and disappointments, as he summarizes in the actions of the "weary psalmist" in "Song for Abraham Klein," who, despite the despair in the world, can sing and thereby remake himself:

Abandoned was the Law,
Abandoned the King.
Unaware he took his instrument,
His habit was to sing.

He sang and nothing changed
Though many heard the song.
But soon his face was beautiful
And soon his limbs were strong. (*Spice-Box* 74)

Leonard Cohen writes not so much to change the world as to understand himself. "What is the expression which the age demands?" he asks in "How to Speak Poetry" in *Death of a Lady's Man* (196). He offers an answer when he suggests that the words themselves, no matter how they are delivered, convey their meaning: "Speak the words with the exact precision with which you would check out a laundry list" (198). For Cohen, writing is a passion that flourishes in adversity. Or, as he explains in *The Favorite Game*, "Poetry is a verdict, not an occupation" (175). "I never felt I was standing at a buffet table. I was reading in the midst of an emergency. I was trying to find comfort or solace," he recently stated, adding that ". . . I don't think we're meant to be entirely consoled in this realm. That's not what this world is about" (qtd. in Stone).

Cohen's impact has been vast. For writers, especially in Canada and Europe, he has demonstrated how neoromanticism, focusing on spiritual and sexual discovery, can establish a wide range of subjects if not of forms. His many attempts at self-discovery may seem repetitive to some, but to his readers they comprise a quest they themselves have undertaken. And in an age when the spiritual is so much in question, Cohen's commitment to such a life remains distinct and appealing. For him, the struggle — prosaically defined as the problems of work, the problems of life — never ends.

Cohen's music remains similarly fixed on the loss of love and of innocence, and the continual decay of society, although recently he admits in the song "Anthem," from *The Future*, "*There is a crack in everything. That's how the light gets in.*" Yet Cohen's developing sound, from electric folk guitar to acoustic guitar and then electronic keyboard and synthesizer of the late eighties, has brought him a new set of fans who intently follow his musical progress. Today, Cohen is thought of first as a musician and second as a writer, an identity not entirely out of touch with his efforts at self-promotion and management. But the recognition by other musicians of his importance is perhaps the greatest measure of his musical talent. A duet with Elton John and cover songs by Judy Collins, Joan Baez, Aaron Neville, Nick Cage, Suzanne Vega, and others underscore his musical impact measured by his switch from writing to singing in 1966–67. A 1991 tribute album, *I'm Your Fan*, by a number of new-wave musicians attests to Cohen's importance as a musical artist, while the prominence of his most recent book, *Stranger Music*, which shot to number three on the Canadian national best-seller list, and a planned Festschrift honouring his sixtieth birthday, confirm his continuing popularity as a writer. He remains a figure of constant fascination, appearing in song lyrics, literary histories, cartoons, musical encyclopaedias, and stage plays.

Of course, Cohen's career has had its highs and lows. Following the success of *The Spice-Box of Earth* in 1961 and the *succès de scandale* of *Beautiful Losers* in 1966, his music in the seventies found little public acceptance. His songs were depressing and filled with intensely felt angst; although he built up a small but solid following, he lost the immediate appeal of a popular singer. Books such as *The Energy of Slaves* and *Book of Mercy*, no matter how strongly written, lost rather than discovered new audiences. Only when *Various Positions* appeared in the mid-eighties, rejected by Cohen's United States record company, Columbia, but a hit in Europe and Canada, did his career slowly begin to recover. Jennifer Warnes's 1986 cover album *Famous Blue Raincoat*, followed by Cohen's immensely successful *I'm Your Man* album two years later, accelerated his reemergence as a major singer, which his album *The Future* (1992) and his book *Stranger Music* (1993) reaffirmed. In his sixtieth year, Cohen has never been more popular, receiving much recognition and many awards. Yet he has hardly slowed down, having just prepared a live album for summer 1994 release and completed a soundtrack for a movie about the Tibetan *Book of the Dead*.

Cohen's life in art is not divorced from his life outside of art — and this account will explore their union. It will also examine the mystique of his popularity and the interplay between his writing and singing against the backdrop of his need to create and its link to spiritual self-discovery. The text attempts to understand not only why there is such a strong and constant interest in Cohen's work but also what compels him to stay on "the front line" of his life. Is the source of his acclaim a postmodern nihilism, lately tinged with modest hope but frequently mixed with depression, or is it his search for spiritual meaning in an age of materialism? Is it the world-weary belief that love is lost and can never be found, or the romantic hope that it is an ideal still to be realized? What this biography modestly offers are some answers to the questions generated by Cohen's life in art.

BEGINNINGS: MONTREAL AND MUSIC

Born in Montreal, September 21, 1934. Studied at McGill and Columbia. Lived in London as a Lord, pursuing the fair, my accent opening the tightest Georgian palaces where I flourished dark and magnificent as Othello. In Oslo where I existed in a Nazi poster. In Cuba the only tourist in Havana, perhaps in the world, where I destroyed my beard on the shores of Varadero, burnt it in nostalgia and anger for the Fidel I used to know. In Greece, where my Gothic insincerities were purged and my style purified under the influence of empty mountains and a foreign mate who cherished simple English. In Montreal, where I always return, scene of the steep streets which support the romantic academies of Canadian Poesy in which I was trained, seat of my family, old as the Indians. More powerful than the Elders of Zion, the last merchants to take blood seriously. I accept money from governments, women, poem sales and, if forced, from employers. I have no hobbies. (Press Release)

Leonard Cohen's arch summary of his life, written in 1963 to publicize his first novel, *The Favorite Game*, is not without truth. Allowing for its hyperbolic prose, it provides a fair, if incomplete, sketch of his life while not diminishing his romantic pretensions, which cynicism will later replace. Emphasizing his Continental rather than Canadian experiences and his triumphs rather than his defeats, Cohen colours his life with travel, politics, drama, love, and tradition, plus the need for cash. But noticeably absent in this mini-biography is his origin and the role and significance of family for him — part of his habit of concealing or revealing certain elements of his life.

Born in Montreal on 21 September 1934 into a Conservative Jewish family — one that claimed ancestors who not only made a mark in European Jewry but also formulated many of the foundations of Montreal Jewry — Cohen had a sustained Jewish childhood. His father was the eldest son of Lyon Cohen, the grandson of Lazarus Cohen, known as Reb Leizer, a teacher in the rabbinical college of Wolozhin, near Wilkovislak in Lithuania. Born in 1844 into a family known for its piety and scholarship in Eastern Europe, Lazarus nonetheless decided to emigrate to Canada in 1869. In 1871 he brought his wife and son Lyon first to Maberly, Ontario, and then to Montreal, which had established the first Jewish community in Canada in 1768. Lazarus quickly developed his business skills, moving from storeowner to lumber merchant to a partnership in the coal industry; finally, he became involved in the dredging business, acquiring other businesses along the way. His brother Hirsch sustained the family's religious traditions, later becoming chief rabbi of Canada.

Lyon displayed similar energy, first in literature. At sixteen he had a four-act play entitled *Esther* produced, and it so impressed the president of the Anglo-Jewish Association that he was asked to become its secretary. He also exerted a Celtic-Scottish influence on the family by speaking English with a Gaelic accent. But Lyon was also involved in business, and by the end of his life he was head of the largest clothing manufacturer in the British dominions, The Freedman Company, which his father had originally acquired. He also served on the boards of the Jewish Public Library, the Montreal Reform Club, the Montreal Insurance Company, the Executive of the Canadian Jewish Congress, and the Zionist Organization of Canada. He founded the *Jewish Times*, later merged with the *Canadian Jewish Chronicle*, and frequently wrote articles for the Jewish press. At thirty-five he became the youngest president of what was then the largest synagogue in Canada, Shaar Hashomayim, its cathedral structure being one of the grandest in the country. He spearheaded the local war effort and encouraged both of his sons to enlist, which they did, becoming the first commissioned Jewish officers in the Canadian army. In September 1924, Lyon Cohen, representing numerous Canadian Jewish organizations, met the pope in Rome, and ten years later, in 1934, the year Leonard Cohen was born, he was again leader of his synagogue.

Nathaniel Bernard Cohen, Lyon's eldest son, was born in 1887; he returned from World War I a partial invalid, although he continued to play an active role in the family's manufacturing business. However, his younger brother, Horace, took more responsibility for these affairs, while another brother, Lawrence, managed the brass works (where the teenage Leonard Cohen was to work one summer). Nineteen years older than his wife Masha, Nathan provided well for his family: a maid, an Irish-Catholic nanny, and a chauffeur-gardener completed the household at 599 Belmont Avenue, Montreal, a large, red-brick, semi-detached house. A reflective, stout man of an imposing nature, Nathan was not a man of letters, although he respected books and passed on to his son an uncut, leather-bound set of the English poets originally given to his father for his bar mitzvah. He was also an avid amateur cameraman whose hobby preserved numerous films of Leonard Cohen and his sister Esther as children and instilled an early interest in photography in his son.

Masha Cohen, born in 1907, came from a family of rabbis. Solomon Klinitsky-Klein, her father, was a rabbi who wrote the *Lexicon of Hebrew Homonyms* and *The Treasury of Rabbinic Interpretations* and who was well known in Canada. Escaping from Poland in 1923, the family moved to Halifax and then to Montreal. However, the family constantly felt the loss of its homeland and traditions, which Cohen's mother, a singer, often recounted in Polish, Russian, or Yiddish. Having corresponded with Lyon Cohen before settling in Montreal, Rabbi Klein and his family quickly met and befriended Cohen's family, and soon Nathan and Masha married.

In the Cohens' three-storey Westmount home, overlooking Murray Hill Park (more formally known as King George VI Park), with Roslyn Junior School and Westmount High nearby, many of the social problems of the Depression did not exist. And while frugality was a familial watchword, the family also enjoyed its privileges, which included a driver and staff. Nathan's Anglophile dress, often an Edwardian attire of spats, monocle, and slicked-down hair, equalled his stern if not reticent behaviour. He relaxed only when listening to music or reading to his children. "Propaganda" in *Flowers for Hitler* provides a glimpse of the man.

Into this world of security and comfort Leonard Norman Cohen was born, his first name continuing the tradition of "L's" (Lazarus, Lyon, Leonard, and Cohen's daughter Lorca, plus his early mentor and close friend Irving Layton) and Norman, the anglicized form of Nehemiah, signifying the rebuilder. His Hebrew name, Elieser, means "God is my help." And, as a Cohen, he is one of the *Kohanim*, a priesthood of succession established, according to the Bible, through Aaron, Moses's brother. But a *ha-kohen* or priest for Israel was a spokesperson for God as well as a lay administrator (*Kohen* means "one who officiates") who, according to tradition, is the first to read the Torah and offer the priestly blessings. A poem in *Parasites of Heaven* entitled "I Am a Priest of God," written in 1966, both accepts and criticizes this role. Cohen, born in the year 5695 in the month of Tishri, according to the Hebrew calendar, constantly examines the powerful and sustained Jewish tradition that saw him as a youth regularly participate in yearly rituals, such as Passover, or weekly ceremonies, such as Shabbat.

Among the most important influences on Cohen, embodying the very traditions of Judaism, was his maternal grandfather Solomon Klinitsky-Klein, who lived with the family and to whom Cohen dedicated, along with his paternal grandmother, Mrs. Lyon Cohen, *The Spice-Box of Earth*. The concluding and longest piece in the collection is the moving prose poem "Lines from My Grandfather's Journal." Reb Klein shared with Cohen numerous legends and stories of Jewish lore. And together they read the book of Isaiah, a formative experience for Cohen because of its Old Testament stress on prophecy and power. His grandfather, whose picture fleetingly appears in the 1965 National Film Board documentary entitled *Ladies and Gentlemen . . . Mr. Leonard Cohen*, was also a writer, but in his forgetfulness he would stop the young Cohen in the house and say, "You are the writer, aren't you?" His question suggested the continuity and tradition between the two, and it was not lost on the younger author.

The concluding poem of *The Spice-Box of Earth* is a tribute to Cohen's grandfather expressed through his grandfather's voice, learned but disillusioned through his remembrance of both Polish and Canadian life. Yet he remarks with wonder that "It is strange that even now prayer is my natural language . . ." (89). In an expression of intensity, the narrating grandfather desires a new purity in the darkness, a purity that his grandson will longingly seek. And even music will provide a form of salvation in an effort to reclaim honesty: "O break down these walls with music. . . . / O come back to our books. / Decorate the Law with human commentary" (90, 92). "Desolation," the narrator laments, "means no angels to wrestle" and the redefinition of tradition. Once "There were beautiful rules: a way to hear thunder, praise a wise man, watch a rainbow, learn of tragedy" (92, 94), but all of that is lost. Nevertheless, "Prayer makes speech a ceremony," and "To observe this ritual in the absence of arks, altars, a listening sky: this is a rich discipline"; the penultimate line, however, is positive: "Lead your priest / from grave to vineyard" (94). This mixture of nostalgia for a lost past and an effort to chart the future is Cohen's recognition of the lasting sense of Jewish tradition that his early life possessed — and which "After the Sabbath Prayers," the second poem in *The Spice-Box of Earth*, confirms.

The peace and security of the family quickly ended with the death of Cohen's father in January 1944. *The Favorite Game* fictionalizes the event, although not the sense of loss that Cohen, then nine, continued to experience. In the novel, Lawrence Breavman thinks of his father as one of the difficult princes of his "private religion, double-natured and arbitrary" (22), while studying a coloured photograph of his father outfitted in "an English suit and all the English reticence that can be woven into cloth" (21–22). Ironically, for the hero, however, "His father's death gave him a touch of mystery, contact with the unknown. He could speak with extra authority on God and Hell" (24). His anger about the death is manifested in his tearing his father's books, ripping up the careful diagrams and colour plates (17). And it finds poignant expression in Breavman's cutting one of his father's bow-ties, sewing a message inside, and then burying it in the garden, an event that actually occurred the day after the funeral (22; Dorman 26). Additionally, Breavman reviews many family movies but mutilates them in protest (5–6), although he also lovingly examines a colour photograph of his father, thereby embodying Cohen's affectionate memories of the father whom he hardly knew but who is remembered in the dedication to his first book, *Let Us Compare Mythologies* (1956).

Cohen begins *Let Us Compare Mythologies* with the moving "Elegy," which is preparation for the more troubling "Rites":

Bearing gifts of flowers and sweet nuts
the family came to watch the eldest son,
my father; and stood about his bed
while he lay on a blood-sopped pillow,
his heart half rotted
and his throat dry with regret.
And it seemed so obvious, the smell so present,
quiet so necessary,
but my uncles prophesied wildly,
promising life like frantic oracles;
and they only stopped in the morning,
after he had died
and I had begun to shout. (22)

Excluded from his *Selected Poems 1956–1968*, the poem painfully recounts the impact and sorrow caused by the death of Cohen's father. The funeral itself Cohen remembers as solemn: his mother unable to join the family until the children were ready to depart from the house; the horrific sight of the lowering coffin; the family's unexpected cheeriness following the *shiva* at the house, with his uncles and aunts around him, his mother alone suffering, while he repressed his feelings. Receptivity became Cohen's strategy: "Having no father I tried to capitalise (on his absence), resolve the Oedipal struggle, (create) good feelings" (qtd. in Dorman 28). His mother (who later remarried unsuccessfully) could repress little and, by necessity, had to rely increasingly on her in-laws for both moral and financial support. Not surprisingly, she also became possessive of Cohen, behaviour he later rejected.

The loss of his father was, for Cohen, an early and unwanted introduction to reality, but it was offset by close friendships with Mike Doddman, Henry Zemel, Henry Moscovitch, Derrik Lyn, Robert Hershorn, Morton Rosengarten, Harold Pascal, Lionel Tiger, and Moses Znaimer (who, in grade seven at Herzliah Junior High School on the edge of Fletcher's Field, would have Irving Layton as his teacher). But Cohen had painfully inherited his father's role, most noticeably at moments of Jewish ritual and ceremony. "And what was it like to have no father?" Lisa asks Breavman, the hero of *The Favorite Game*. "It made you more grown-up. You carved the chicken, you sat where he sat," he replies (24). At McGill, one of Cohen's surviving essays is on death; ironically, Cohen emphasizes the lack of its effect on him, although he concludes by reversing that attitude: "Death is a tragedy and whether it strikes at an eight-year-old youngster . . . or a senile old man, a scar is always left on one . . . of the survivors — a scar that does not heal quickly" (qtd. in Dorman 48–49). Later, he would write that "A scar is what happens when the word is made flesh" (*Favorite Game* 3).

Death, of course, is a theme throughout Cohen's work, whether it is Edith's suicide under the elevator in *Beautiful Losers* or the spiritual deaths recounted in *Death of a Lady's Man*, a work dedicated to the memory of his mother. The tragic deaths of influential figures such as Federico García Lorca, murdered near Granada in 1936, and of friends such as the Montreal Hispanic, who taught the teenaged Cohen three guitar lessons before he suddenly committed suicide, or Steve Smith, the dedicatee of *Beautiful Losers*, surrounded him. And with death comes anger, as in "The Lover After All":

> You die exactly in that attitude of scorn, you filthy parasite of the worthless ordeal. You die looking exactly like that, in all constipated possession of your high degree. . . .
>
> A white butterfly flickers like the end of a home movie, and it gives me words, and with them I can make a world for you to hustle in, a large world, complex and true, where I turn out to be the lover after all, and you turn out to be merely stupid, but forgiven in a hail of seeds. (*Death of a Lady's Man* 66)

For Cohen, life after the death of his father took, at least on the surface, a conventional form. His Scottish terrier kept him company until it disappeared one winter, ill, and was not found until nearly spring, a traumatic event for the young boy. He continued his education at Roslyn Junior School, a short walk from his home, where sports and studies balanced each other, although Cohen, a bright student, easily found himself bored with the routine. At the same time, he attended the Shaar Hashomayim Hebrew school attached to the synagogue, and, at the early age of six, he felt in touch with the language and imagery of the Bible in both English and Hebrew. But the raging world war, and an awareness of Jewish suffering, provided a further deepening of his sense of loss. He later remarked that his true education began in 1945 when he first saw concentration-camp pictures (Dorman 362).

In 1947, his thirteenth year, Cohen had his bar mitzvah, saddened, of course, by the absence of his father despite the efforts of his many relatives and the celebratory party held at his grandmother's home. His Hebrew education continued at the synagogue, however, as his grandfather's presence and reputation increased, and Cohen's knowledge of Hebrew scripture expanded. However, his growing scepticism of the religion may have originated in his resentment against God for the loss of his father and the consequent anguish that he, his mother, and his sister suffered. During this period, his love of solitude also emerged, and he often ran home after school to write rather than play ball with his friends. This interest coincided with an encouragement for literature by one of his English teachers, Mr. Waring. Later, at Westmount High, from which Cohen would graduate in 1951 at the age of sixteen (in Quebec, Canadian secondary education ends with grade eleven), he was elected to the board of publishers and the student council. And linked to his desire to write was a determination to understand how, as a descendant of Aaron, he could fulfil his calling as *Kohen*, a high priest.

In 1949, at the age of fifteen, Cohen came upon a book of poetry by Lorca, a writer whose brooding vision and powerful verse, Cohen ironically said, "ruined" his life (qtd. in Dorman 36). But Lorca was, and remains, a seminal influence on Cohen: as poet, performer, and artist, Lorca — killed quite literally by twentieth-century politics (he was executed on 19 August 1936, shortly after his arrest by Spanish partisans following his return to Spain to aid in the Civil War) — has stood as a representative artist for Cohen. Lorca's fanciful belief that he possessed the blood of gypsies and Jews enhanced Cohen's identification with him. His elegiac tone, faith in a spiritual absolute, and struggle between the artist and society echo throughout Cohen's work. And a question of Lorca's remains central to Cohen's work: *"What stigma has passion placed on my brow?"* (*Collected Poetry* xxv).

Lorca's transcendental vision "taught me that poetry can be pure and profound, and at the same time popular," Cohen told a Spanish journalist (qtd. in Dorman 37). He also identified with Lorca's surrealism and his qualified use of dreams as a technique.

23

Cohen understood with Lorca that while such an evasion may be pure, it is often not clear. "We Latins," explains Lorca, "want sharp profiles and visible mystery. Form and sensuality" (*Poet* xvii). This statement, in Lorca's 1928 lecture "Imagination, Inspiration, Evasion," represents equally well Cohen's aesthetic. His naming his daughter Lorca attests to Lorca's abiding influence not only on Cohen's songs and poems but also on his life.

Cohen began writing poetry seriously in 1950 at sixteen (Lorca was seventeen when he began writing poetry). It occurred, Cohen recalls, while he was

> sitting down at a card table on a sun porch one day when I decided to quit a job. I was working in a brass foundry [his uncle Lawrence's, called W.R. Cuthbert] at the time and one morning I thought, I just can't take this anymore, and I went out to the sun porch and I started a poem. I had a marvelous sense of mastery and power, and freedom, and strength, when I was writing this poem. ("Leonard Cohen: The Poet" 30; the foundry appears in *Favorite Game* 110–12)

But he also maintained an interest in sports: cycling, skiing, sailing, and hockey, playing for the school team. And, of course, in women. The only sensation from this period that he recalls, Cohen has wryly commented, was one of persistent desire. He also developed a modest skill as a teenage hypnotist, a talent that Breavman exploits when he hypnotizes Heather, the Breavmans' maid, in *The Favorite Game* (51–55).

On 31 May 1949, Cohen was one of seven graduates from the afternoon Hebrew school he had been attending at Shaar Hashomayim Synagogue (its president was his uncle, Horace Cohen, OBE), and he was chosen to offer the opening Hebrew prayer as well as to participate in the presentation entitled "What Is Torah?" Although Cohen did well in the school, he did not win any of the scholastic prizes.

Attending summer camp was one of Cohen's more popular activities, and at Camp Hiawatha in the Laurentians he first met his long-time friend, Morton Rosengarten, a year older. Like

Cohen, who played the piano and guitar (the latter always accompanied him), Mort was musical, although he played the banjo and trombone. He became a part of the Cohen household, witnessing Mrs. Cohen's deep attachment to her son and the way that she, from a Russian village, was at odds with her "classy" in-laws. She was often the source, as was her father, of the mythology of the family and its past, which entranced Cohen according to Rosengarten. The two friends shared two years at McGill and remained close for many years after as Mort became a sculptor and artist and Cohen turned to writing and songs. Krantz in *The Favorite Game* is a fictionalized version of Rosengarten.

As well as girls, summer camp offered Cohen music, although it was often only an introduction to the more transparent forms of folk singing. Irving Morton, a folk singer and leftist, taught Cohen a number of songs while he was at a socialist camp in 1950. In the extended camp scenes in *The Favorite Game*, the hero quite naturally entertains the campers with his guitar playing. Breavman's playing, plus the Hebrew singing on the Sabbath, lead to his wish to be "the gentle hero the folk come to love, . . . the Baal Shem Tov who carried children piggy-back" (203). Cohen's early introduction to music came at home when his father played the singer Sir Harry Lauder and the operas of Gilbert and Sullivan. Among his earliest musical influences, in addition to what he heard at home, were national anthems and colonial folk songs, often sung at school or heard on the radio, plus the flamenco guitar music of Spain. Jazz and pop also became important to him, and for many years his idol was Ray Charles (the subject of the movie that Krantz and Edith watch in *Beautiful Losers*). Early piano lessons with Miss McDougall, which did not go very far, were soon supplanted by guitar and clarinet lessons, the latter leading to Cohen's membership in the high-school marching band.

At seventeen Cohen also formed a country-and-western band, called The Buckskin Boys, with his childhood friend Mike Doddman, who played harmonica, and a friend of Doddman's known only as Terry, who played bass. The name originated in the curious fact that all three owned buckskin jackets, Cohen having inherited his from his father. Barn dancing or square dancing was their specialty, with Cohen playing an amplified rhythm guitar. The band performed often at high schools, church basements, and dances, surviving from 1951 to 1954 while its members were in university. Its success also proved that Cohen had a gift for performing, being natural (although also nervous) on stage.

Poetry and music did not compete for Cohen's attention because his earliest poetry contained the basic structures and qualities of song. The two have always coexisted, although his interest in music may predate his interest in poetry. However, as Cohen has reiterated in various interviews, they developed simultaneously: "I was interested in the kind of language that went well with the guitar." Importantly, he claims that "words are completely empty and any emotion can be poured into them." "Almost all my songs can be sung any way. They can be sung as tough songs or as gentle songs or as contemplative songs or as courting songs" ("Leonard Cohen: The Poet" 26). And although he sings in "Tower of Song" from *I'm Your Man* that "I was born with the gift of a golden voice" — a line that always brings cheers at his concerts — Cohen has also confessed that "There are only about four notes I can claim with a certain authority. I've never had the luxury of the buffet table" (qtd. in Walsh 39). Winning the 1993 Juno Award for Canadian Male Vocalist of the Year prompted Cohen ironically to remark, "It's only in a country like this that I could get the male vocalist of the year" (qtd. in McCann).

"HOW TO SPEAK POETRY" — AND OTHER THINGS

Leonard Cohen registered at McGill University on 21 September 1951, his seventeenth birthday, entering Jewish for his nationality on the registration form. At five feet eight inches, he had reached

FIGURE 2

*The Buckskin Boys: a country-and-western or barn-dance band
formed by Cohen and friends during his days at McGill.*

his full height and looked every bit the enthusiastic, if slightly pudgy, undergraduate. Founded in 1821, McGill had long established its reputation as the premier English-speaking university in Quebec and a necessary step for entering English-Quebec culture. The university, while not maintaining an announced quota system, nonetheless carefully monitored the number of Jews attending. On his entrance exam, taken the previous June, Cohen had averaged 74.1%, English literature being his lowest mark at 57%. His highest marks were in math. His McGill performance overall was average, although in his final year he achieved a first-class standing in English and won the Chester MacNaughton Prize for Creative Writing and the Peterson Memorial Prize in literature. In his first year he studied arts; in his second he studied commerce, which included accounting, commercial law, and political science; in his final two years he focused again on arts. Cohen describes the completion of his work at McGill as paying "off old debts to my family and to my society," but if there had been support for dropping out, he would have done so ("Leonard Cohen: The Poet" 27). Indecisive about a career when he graduated at twenty in 1955, he was gently pressured to consider the family business, succeeding his father, although his preference was for writing and music.

Cohen's extracurricular activities at McGill included membership in the Zeta Beta Tau fraternity, of which he became president, presenting unorthodox proposals such as keeping its membership exclusively Jewish and drinking on the lawn of the fraternity house. This stunt led to his impeachment, accelerated by his conducting meetings to the accompaniment of his guitar and conspiring to sneak a girl into the fraternity's gathering dressed in her boyfriend's coat; she startled the assembly when at a signal she removed the coat to cast a naked vote. Such pranks, however, did not prevent Cohen from being elected president of the McGill Debating Union Society in 1954. His carefully crafted acceptance speech was a satire on businessmen in the guise of an argument for the separation of Quebec because "foreigners in Ottawa" were mistreating it: the time had come, he declared, to "quit the Confederation, consolidate and centralise our own power." Who was to lead this new entity? A businessman. Rejecting the lawyer, who is "a deceptive sophist half smothered in ipso factos," and the "artsman," who is "an antique fossil and at best will make a fine filing clerk," Cohen proposed that the businessman alone could take the province forward, citing Proverbs 22.29 to clinch his argument (qtd. in Dorman 59–60). Impatient, however, with the inactivity and prolonged executive meetings of the society, Cohen acted by banning any further meetings or debates.

Among Cohen's professors at McGill was F.R. Scott, who taught him commercial law and who convinced him to enter, for a short while, the Faculty of Law, believing that Cohen could pursue a career as a writer and lawyer. Scott, recognized as the *seigneur* of the Montreal school of poetry, was also a distinguished constitutional law scholar. His influence on Cohen was direct, and he quickly sensed Cohen's literary talent. For Cohen, visits to the Scotts were "warm and wonderful [with] a very open fluid atmosphere; lots of fun; drinking; and talk of politics and poetry" (qtd. in Djwa 288). In turn, the Scotts ventured into downtown Montreal clubs to hear Cohen sing and read. Cohen was also invited to North Hatley to stay with the Scotts at their summer cottage, and they encouraged him to write by inviting him to stay at the lean-to cabin of Scott's brother, Elton, farther up the lake. In 1957, in fact, Cohen began to write *The Spice-Box of Earth* there, and in 1958 he visited the cabin to work on *The Favorite Game*. He acknowledges the importance of Scott and his offer of a retreat in "Summer Haiku *For Frank and Marian Scott*," in *The Spice-Box of Earth* (76–77). Cohen actually carved the poem into a rock that, when presented to the Scotts, found use as a doorstop at the summer house (Djwa 289). Scott's support of Cohen extended to a recommendation for a Canada Council grant.

Cohen's contact with Scott continued through the sixties, often introducing him to new poetic and musical voices. For example, at an 8 January 1966 all-day poetry party that Scott

FIGURE 3

Cohen as president of the McGill Debating
Union Society (first row, second from the left).

organized, with Irving Layton, Louis Dudek, Al Purdy, A.J.M. Smith, and Ralph Gustafson present, Cohen brought out his guitar and raved about the new poet of America, Bob Dylan. No one had heard of him, so Scott rushed out, bought two of his records, and began to play them. Only Cohen could tolerate the sound; Purdy, according to Scott, "bounded out of the room as though booted from behind," shouting " 'It's an awful bore. I can't listen to any more of this' " (qtd. in Djwa 290). Cohen nonetheless announced that there was an audience out there waiting for him and that *he* would be the Canadian Dylan, a claim that none of them thought serious enough to refute. They spent the afternoon of the party watching two NFB films: *A.M. Klein: The Poet as Landscape* and *Ladies and Gentlemen . . . Mr. Leonard Cohen*, which Cohen declined to view. By 10 p.m. Scott had offered to play one of the Dylan records again, and this time dancing, not criticism, was the result.

At McGill Cohen generally avoided lectures: "I yearned to live a semi-bohemian lifestyle, an unstructured life; but a *consecrated* one; some kind of calling," Cohen noted about this period (qtd. in Dorman 61). Rather than focusing on academic topics, Cohen pursued various interests from zoology to political science and, of course, English. At that time, the McGill English department had two well-known members: Hugh MacLennan — whose novel *Two Solitudes* had rocked Canada when it appeared in 1945, and who began part-time teaching at McGill the year that Cohen entered — and Louis Dudek — a Canadian-born, European-centred poet with a recent PhD from Columbia University. Cohen took classes from both men: Canadian literature from MacLennan, and, from Dudek, "Great Writers of Europe, 1850 to the Present" (a survey course beginning with the Enlightenment and ending with romanticism in the first year, and beginning with naturalism and ending with modernism in the second). Cohen also studied twentieth-century poetry and drama.

One of Cohen's final programs was the advanced course in creative writing, under the direction of MacLennan, which required the submission of work before acceptance into the course. MacLennan and Cohen liked each other, the older writer often corresponding with the younger after he left McGill. Dudek also offered "The Art of Poetry," but Cohen did not take it; he did, however, learn a great deal about European and twentieth-century poetry from Dudek in "Modern Poetry," a year-long course that Cohen took in 1954. Dudek also championed Ezra Pound, often over Cohen's objections. Dudek had begun to correspond with Pound at St. Elizabeths and would later publish their exchange in *Dk/Some Letters of Ezra Pound*. But W.B. Yeats and Lorca were more to Cohen's taste, and he read widely in both.

Dudek was involved in another activity at McGill in addition to teaching: initiating and editing the McGill Poetry Series, "the first venture of its kind in Canada," whose purpose was "to present to the university community and the public the work of young writers at McGill of outstanding ability," as the statement reads in its first publication, Cohen's *Let Us Compare Mythologies* (6). Its appearance relates to the now-famous "knighting" incident, which occurred in October 1954. In the second or third week of the "Modern Poetry" course, Cohen showed Dudek some of his poetry, which Dudek quickly recognized as being of little merit. Two weeks later, however, Cohen showed him more, and in "The Sparrows" Dudek spotted a poem of promise. As they walked down one of the corridors in the arts-faculty building, Dudek impulsively commanded Cohen to kneel. With the manuscript in his hand, Dudek "knighted" Cohen "poet," then permitted him to rise, one of the more pseudodramatic or seriocomic episodes in the history of Canadian literature. Cohen had joined a new order and was allowed to participate in its debates, readings, workshops, and publications.

A consequence of this event was Cohen's involvement with the journal *CIV/n*, which began to publish in mimeograph form 250 copies in January 1953; it lasted two years, producing seven issues. The unusual title originated when Dudek saw a statement of Pound's: "CIV/n [Pound's abbreviation for civilization] — not a one-man job," which was reprinted at the beginning of every issue. Civilization requires the efforts of many, emulated by those who worked for, and contributed to, the magazine. Aileen Collins (later to marry Dudek) edited, and Dudek and Layton were editorial advisors, which actually meant that the three, and sometimes more, sat around and argued over what to print and what to cut.

The fourth issue of the little magazine contains Cohen's two earliest publications, "An Halloween Poem to Delight My Younger Friends (Où sont les jeunes?)" (8) and "Poème en Prose" (13), which appear alongside work by Cid Corman, Phyllis Webb, Dudek, Robert Creeley, Layton, and Raymond Souster. Cohen's name is printed as "Leonard Norman Cohen," and the author's note tellingly reads: "Leonard N. Cohen . . . composes poetry to the guitar; now studying at McGill" (22). The second poem begins: "The river confronted us, the Charles, and through it's [sic] secret undulations swarmed the shadows of ten dozen streetlamps and a moon"; retitled and revised, it appears as "Friends" in *Let Us Compare Mythologies* (37). The same issue of *CIV/n* contains a long section on Pound, including Dudek's "Why Is Ezra Pound Being Held in St. Elizabeths Hospital, Washington, D.C.?" Four other poems by Cohen, including "The Sparrows," appeared in *CIV/n* before it stopped publication in the winter of 1955.

Just as important for the young poet was the literary circle that emerged around the magazine and brought him into contact with more experienced (if not older) and equally "revolutionary" writers who sought to challenge the poetic orthodoxy of the country; or, as Aileen Collins later remarked, to contradict the Canadian Authors' Association notion of poetry as a blend of maple syrup (qtd. in Dorman 62) — at least as seen from Montreal. This group included Irving Layton, Betty Sutherland (sister of the McGill poet John Sutherland and with whom Layton had been living since the mid-1940s and had married in 1948), the sculptor Buddy Rozynski, art director of the magazine, and, later, Phyllis Webb, Doug Jones, Eli Mandel, Raymond Souster, F.R. Scott, Cid Corman, Robert Creeley, and Charles Olson.

The coffeehouse culture at this time also provided an outlet for Cohen, supplanting the university with its air of bohemia and experimentation. Café André, near the McGill students'-union building, often became the unofficial headquarters of Cohen, Rosengarten, and others. Called "The Shrine" and located in an old house, Café André became a centre for the poet-troubadour, who also frequented locations on Stanley Street and Mountain Street, in a scene so underground, he once commented, that it lacked "subversive intentions because even that would be beneath it" ("Leonard Cohen" [Sony] [3]). Cohen was involved in this scene partly because he recoiled from what the narrator in *The Favorite Game* calls "the uglifying extravagance to which Westmount Jews and Gentiles are currently devoted" (29). Cohen's family thought he would grow out of it, but he surprised them by turning his back on a career in business, to the disappointment of his uncles. As he declares in "Alexander Trocchi, Public Junkie, Priez pour Nous," his decision was perceived as ". . . treachery / to the men's clothing industry" (*Flowers* 46). Cohen persisted in his independence, even renting an apartment with Rosengarten on Lower Stanley Street, a private space away from the university and his family.

The English-language writing scene in Montreal at this time was minuscule. In the mid-fifties, writing poetry garnered little prestige and few prizes. And no *girls*, as Cohen recently reminisced. "But a few of us were on fire and we'd write for each other and any girl that would listen" (qtd. in Sharp 79). One of those burning with poetic intensity, and a central figure in sustaining and extending Cohen's life as a poet, was Irving Layton, whom Cohen had met briefly in 1949 and again in 1954 at a poetry workshop at McGill. Layton, at this time shifting between being a flamboyant schoolteacher at Herzliah Junior High School, a part-time lecturer in literature at Sir George Williams University, and a teaching assistant in political science at McGill, was also a pugnacious poet who had already published two books. He quickly began to have a decisive influence on Cohen, demonstrating the value of the prophetic or satiric voice over the lyrical or historical. This division would later create a conflict for Cohen between Dudek's focus on discipline and knowledge and Layton's earthiness and Dionysian character, which Dudek found vulgar and contrary to high modernist ideals. However, during the early fifties, as Cohen was participating in the literary debates surrounding *CIV/n*, Layton and Dudek shared a similar desire to reform Canadian poetry, not the least through satire, with Westmount often the subject of their criticism.

Layton had published his first book, *Here and Now*, in 1945, his second in 1948. In 1954, the year Cohen remet him, Layton had two more books appear, one being the important *The Long Pea-Shooter*. More significant for Cohen, perhaps, was the encounter with an energetic, egocentric writer who celebrated not only language but also the life of a poet, which he transmitted through the country via ebullient readings that challenged complacency and books that defied indifference. "Now with a happy / screech he bounded from monument to monument / in their most consecrated plots, . . ." Cohen writes in his tribute, "For My Old Layton" (*Flowers* 37). Proletarian, passionate, and patriotic, Layton's presence galvanized Cohen into poetic action. Dudek had knighted him, but Layton kicked him in the pants.

Politics, sex, violence, religion, cruelty — all are topics in Layton's audacious and voluminous poetry, which constantly celebrates creation. Polite verse was out; prophecy was in. Streetwise and worldly, Layton encouraged the Dionysian in Cohen and pushed him to explore his art while treating it with respect. Yet their learning was reciprocal: "I taught him how to dress; he taught me how to live forever," Cohen declared (qtd. in Dorman 57). Cohen often accompanied Layton on reading, promotional, or conference tours and made frequent trips with him to Toronto, where, on one occasion, they read at the old Greenwich Gallery on Bay Street. Don Owen, the filmmaker, recalls how Cohen "always seemed to leave the gallery with the most interesting woman there, the one I'd spent all evening trying to get up enough nerve to say hello to" (31). These feats were all the more remarkable because, according to Owen, Cohen was in his pudgy phase, which he would grow out of when he went to Greece.

Layton became Cohen's exuberant mentor and guide, which the opening of "Last Dance at the Four Penny" makes clear (the Four Penny, which Cohen and three partners operated for a short time, was an art gallery in which every door frame was painted a different colour):

Layton, when we dance our freilach
under the ghostly handkerchief,
the miracle rabbis of Prague and Vilna
resume their sawdust thrones,
and angels and men, asleep so long
in the cold palaces of disbelief,
gather in sausage-hung kitchens
to quarrel deliciously and debate
the sounds of the Ineffable Name. (*Spice-Box* 71)

Celebrating inspiration, debate, and the prophetic tradition of Judaism united Layton and Cohen in a quest to return emotion to poetry by breaking out of modernism's discipline, order, and restricting conservatism of subject matter and form. Poems such as "Song," beginning with "When with lust I am smitten," and "It Swings, Jocko" in *The Spice-Box of Earth* present this quest.

But as life at McGill and beyond grew in richness, Westmount still had a hold on Cohen — most noticeably through his grand-father, whose health was declining, and his mother. After his grandfather died, Cohen's mother remarried, and the poet began to understand more clearly the limitations of his Montreal back-ground:

He had thought that his tall uncles in their dark clothes were princes of an élite brotherhood. He had thought the synagogue was their house of purification. He had thought their businesses were realms of feudal benevolence. But he had grown to understand that none of them even pretended to these things. They were proud of their financial and communal success. They liked to be first, to be respected, to sit close to the altar, to be called up to lift the scrolls. They weren't pledged to any other idea. They did not believe their blood was consecrated. Where had he got the notion that they did? . . .

No, his uncles were not grave enough. They were strict, not grave. (*Favorite Game* 126)

Coupled with his newly discovered acceptance as a poet, Cohen's rejection of Westmount provided the confidence to begin the first of many exoduses from Montreal. They took Cohen first to New York but eventually to England, Greece, and the United States, although he always maintained a home in Montreal. But spiritual as well as physical restlessness never permitted him to stay in one place for very long.

LET US COMPARE MYTHOLOGIES

Following his 1955 graduation from McGill, accomplished only by writing supplemental exams and getting no more than 50% on them, according to Cohen ("Leonard Cohen: The Poet" 27), he faced two options: join his uncles in their various enterprises to ease the financial burden on his widowed mother, or pursue the semibohemian life he was enjoying among the writers and artists of Montreal. He more or less spent a year considering these alternatives while attending law school for a term and planning and promoting his first book, *Let Us Compare Mythologies*, composed largely of work that he had written between the ages of fifteen and twenty.

In the wake of the 1955 Kingston, Ontario, conference on Canadian writing, and the close of Contact Press, Dudek thought of a new outlet for young poets with the imprimatur of a university: the McGill Poetry Series. The emergence of the series at this time could not have been more propitious for Cohen, although he was at first a reluctant contributor. Organized through a rejuvenated Contact Press and set up by Dudek, Souster, and Layton, the series published ten books between 1956 and 1966, including work by Daryl Hine, David Solway, Pierre Coupey, and, of course, Cohen. Its purpose was to give poets of promise at McGill an outlet for their work. But when Dudek offered to publish Cohen's work first, Cohen "was slow and reluctant to present his manuscript for editing"; in fact, Dudek never saw the completed manuscript of *Let Us Compare Mythologies* until it was published. Part of the reason was Cohen's resistance to Dudek's rejection of "the sentimental late-romantic tradition in poetry," to which Cohen was attached in rebellion against the pull toward modernism expressed by Dudek and others and vividly enacted in the work of Pound, Williams, and Olson (Dudek, letter).

Cohen himself arranged for a printer and bookbinder, Mr. Greenspoon, and masterminded the entire production of the book, taking responsibility for its design, typesetting, production, paper, and printing. His friend Freda Guttman prepared illustrations, and he paid three hundred dollars to have the work hardbound, not softbound as Dudek had originally envisioned. Cohen also took to distributing the book, selling it on campus and in cafés and bookstores, although he also took subscriptions for it, which made printing the approximately four hundred copies possible. Ads were also placed in the *McGill Daily*.

Cohen wrote the forty-four poems in the seventy-nine-page volume roughly between 1949 and 1954 and published the book at age twenty-two. The poems confront a series of themes characteristic of late adolescence: loss and discovery, faith and doubt, love and its disappearance. Signalling the cross between romantic poetry and modern writing is the volume's epigraph, from the fourth section of William Faulkner's "The Bear," in which Ike McCaslin quotes the concluding two lines from the second stanza of John Keats's "Ode on a Grecian Urn" (*Let Us Compare* 11). In addition to emphasizing the difference between the rhetorical and the prosaic, the passage clarifies the permanence of truth and its union with beauty — and why, after four years of hunting, Ike cannot kill the bear. Immediately after the section that Cohen cites, Faulkner has McCaslin say, *"He was talking about truth. Truth is one. It doesn't change. It covers all things which touch the heart . . ."* (29). This passage suggests the ideal in, and purpose of, Cohen's book. The conversation in Faulkner occurs during a scene that emphasizes inheritance, patrimony, history, and desire, themes that Cohen stresses in his book. As well, references to Tennyson and Rossetti in "Ballad" reflect his interest in nineteenth-century poets, while mythology united with religious sensuality appears in "Prayer for Messiah," "Saviors," and "Exodus."

Let Us Compare Mythologies contains other themes that inform Cohen's later poetry: Jewish persecution, especially in the Holocaust ("Lovers"), sexuality and the attraction to women ("When This American Woman"), lyrical sensuality ("On Certain Incredible Nights"), anger ("Letter"), culture and its impact ("Satan in Westmount"), cityscapes reflecting the darkness of life and religion ("Saint Catherine Street"; "Beside the Shepherd"), and in "Pagans," ironic frustration with art or history in resolving crises:

Dear friend, I have searched all night
    through each burnt paper,
but I fear I will never find
the formula to let you die. (45)

Despite the imitation of Victorian stanzas, as well as a surfeit of Swinburnian imagery, Cohen also experiments, especially with the prose poem and surrealist imagery. "Friends" is an unsuccessful example of the first, marking his early interest in a form later developed in *Parasites of Heaven* and *Book of Mercy*. "Halloween Poem," his first published poem, is a more accomplished blend of poetry and prose. Representing surrealism in the book is "Prayer for Sunset," which unites many of the themes Cohen addresses:

The sun is tangled
  in black branches,
raving like Absalom
  between sky and water,
struggling through the dark terebinth
to commit its daily suicide. (49)

Let Us Compare Mythologies, while a young poet's first work designed to shock as well as excite ("The moon dangling wet like a half-plucked eye" in "Summer Night," for instance [54]), also contains many subjects that Cohen would later enlarge. It is a prototype of the confrontations and challenges that he later addresses through more extended and elaborate means, as if he were returning to this book to annotate and expand its many troubling topics, but with more precise language and more exact thoughts. Cohen's first book also provides glimpses of his using poetry as a form of prayer and the role of the poet as a sacred, if not a prophetic, voice.

Cohen began to get exposure: the record *Six Montreal Poets*, recorded by the Canadian Broadcasting Corporation in 1956 and released by Folkways Records in the United States in 1957, placed him in the company of his predecessors — Layton, F.R. Scott, A.M. Klein, A.J.M. Smith, and Dudek. Produced by the soon-to-be impresario, Sam Gesser, who brought people such as Pete Seeger and the Weavers to Montreal, the album marked Cohen as the most important young poet in Montreal. Eight poems from his book appear on *Six Montreal Poets*, including "The Sparrows" and "Elegy." Scott's album notes list Cohen as the author of a second book of poetry, *The Spice-Box of Earth* (not published until 1961), and a novel, "A Ballet of Lepers," which remains unpublished.

The opportunity to study at Columbia University in New York in 1956–57 — where Dudek had received his PhD in 1951 and Lorca had briefly studied English in 1929 — could not be resisted. Enrolling in the School of General Studies, Cohen arrived in New York in the fall of 1956 and took up residence at International House on Morningside Drive. He gave some brief thought to law school but quickly realized that, unlike Scott and Klein, he could not join law with literature. Poetry was his purpose, and he soon began to associate with writers and singers in the Columbia bohemian scene. At this time, the Beats began to find an audience, which the reception of Allen Ginsberg's *Howl and Other Poems* (1956) accelerated. Ginsberg, also a Columbia graduate, excited many in New York with his famous 13 October 1955 reading of "Howl" at Gallery Six, a converted auto-repair shop. Jack Kerouac was in the audience; two months later, his own work, *On the Road*, was accepted by Viking for publication, although the book did not appear until 1957. The sudden prominence of Lawrence Ferlinghetti, Gregory Corso, Gary Snyder, and William S. Burroughs confirmed the value of counterculture writing as their work received both condemnation and praise. Their radical confrontation with social conservatism and enervation confirmed for Cohen the importance of his antiestablishment stance. The shocking voices of the Beats extended the aesthetic that Layton, and before him Lorca, had celebrated.

Sections of *The Favorite Game* incorporate Cohen's New York adventures and share Lorca's scepticism about the city when he attended Columbia. "How can anybody take the skyscrapers seriously? Breavman wonders. And what if they lasted ten thousand years, and what if the world spoke American? Where was the comfort for today?" (149). These are troubling questions for the young narrator, whose independence is threatened: "Where was his ordeal?" he wonders (149). Leaning out his window at the World Student House, Breavman "watches the sun ignite the Hudson. It is no longer the garbage river, catch-all for safes, excrement, industrial poison . . ." (149–50). What he seeks is grander: "There must be something written on the fiery water. An affidavit from God. A detailed destiny chart. The address of his perfect wife. A message choosing him for glory or martyrdom" (150). In New York, Cohen searched for a similar clue through coffeehouses, bookstores, and new relationships.

Returning in 1957 to Montreal, Cohen pursued his literary contacts. In June he joined Layton, Earle Birney, and Jay Macpherson for an unexpected visit to Anne Wilkinson to announce the birth of *Delta* to replace *CIV/n*. During that visit, Layton took Cohen for lunch with E.J. Pratt, the meeting arranged for them by Birney. By July Cohen had completed a draft of his first and still unpublished novel, "A Ballet of Lepers," and was working on a new book of poems. He gave his first professional poetry recital at Dunn's Birdland, a room above Dunn's Famous Steak House on Ste. Catherine Street in Montreal. Working with a pianist and arranger named Maury Kaye, who had a twelve- or fifteen-piece band on the small stage, Cohen started reciting his poetry at midnight, often improvising while Kaye played either his own or other tunes on the piano. Occasionally Cohen would read set pieces such as "The Gift," from *The Spice-Box of Earth* (3). The gig lasted about a month; then Cohen worked with a Winnipeg guitarist, Lenny Breau, for the rest of 1957 and into 1958 (Ruhlmann 12).

While attending Columbia University, Cohen heard Kerouac give poetry readings over jazz at the Village Vanguard, inspiring him to do the same in Montreal. He also began to appear at the Tokai and hung out at well-known coffeehouses on Stanley Street and other haunts such as the Pam-Pam and the McGill Union, now the McCord Museum on Sherbrooke Street. Supplementing his readings was his own guitar accompaniment.

At this time Cohen's close relationship with Layton meant acting as the best man at Layton's faux wedding in the spring of 1958. Layton, who would not ask his wife, Betty Sutherland Layton, for a divorce, agreed to buy his new love, Aviva Cantor, a wedding ring. Cohen, dressed for the occasion, joined Layton and Aviva for lunch; afterward they visited an exclusive jewellery shop on Mountain Street where she selected several gold bands. Neglecting her, Layton found a chunky silver bracelet for Betty. Cohen took the gold band and placed it on Aviva's finger to assuage Layton's callous behaviour. Aviva called herself Mrs. Layton from that moment on, much to Layton's dislike.

Recalling the incident, Cohen said that Layton "probably felt like living with both women. I think he could have handled them both, too. It was the *women* who demanded a resolution" (qtd. in Cameron, *Irving Layton* 277).

That year *The McGill Chapbook* contained three of Cohen's poems: "Now of Sleeping," "It Swings, Jocko," and "Song to Make Me Still." Interestingly, Cohen gives his birthday as "b. 5695 (Hebrew Calendar)," thereby asserting his Jewish identity. One of his most memorable encounters with the literary past was a visit to A.M. Klein in June 1959. Cohen, affected by this meeting, wrote "Song for Abraham Klein," published in *The Spice-Box of Earth* (74). The poem registers Cohen's belief in the ability of art to renew and of poetic song to comfort; years later, in 1964, Cohen cited Klein frequently in a lecture entitled "Loneliness and History."

The importance of Klein for Cohen has been underestimated, for, next to Layton, he is Cohen's most significant Canadian model. A student at McGill and later, in 1946, a visiting lecturer in English there, Klein began to appear in the first generation of important Canadian modernist journals: *Preview*, *First Statement*, and *Northern Review*. He also quickly developed a distinctive voice that is at once Jewish and Canadian. The bitter irony in Cohen's early poems, such as "Lovers" in *Let Us Compare Mythologies*, is reminiscent of Klein. Both use similar poetic and rhetorical tricks and rely on exotic words, worlds, and biblical diction in their poetry. There is also a similar irony about one's self and childhood heroism, while understatement, mixing a kind of surrealism and bathos (represented in Klein's "Upon the Heavenly Scarp"), also appears in Cohen. The opening of Klein's "Reb Levi Yitschok talks to God" nicely anticipates the sudden shifts of tone and diction found in Cohen's various works:

Reb Levi Yitschok, crony of the Lord,
Familiar of heaven, broods these days.
His heart erupts in sighs. He will have a word
At last, with Him of the mysterious ways.

He will go to the synagogue of Berditchev,
And there sieve out his plaints in a dolorous sieve. (146)

But despite the raging, the pleading, the cajoling, the singing of Reb Levi, he remains unanswered by God "even when the sunshine smiled" (147).

Klein established not only a tone but also a subject for Cohen — traditional Judaism — and showed him how it could work poetically. Furthermore, Klein wrote fiction as well as poetry, proving to the young writer that he need not be wedded to a single genre and that history, as well as startling time shifts, could be managed in a single text. "Divinely he sang the scriptured note," Klein begins "Reader of the Scroll," only to transform the tone from celebration to accusation:

For in a single breath to hiss
The ten outrageous names of those
Who on the Persian gallows rose —
Oh this was pleasure, joyance this! (121–22)

Lyrics of eroticism ("Love"), poems of Quebec ("The Rocking Chair"), celebrations of Montreal ("Montreal"), critiques of Judaism ("And the Man Moses Was Meek"), poems of sorrow ("Five Weapons against Death"), prayer ("Stance of the Amidah"), and the role of the poet ("Portrait of the Poet as Landscape"): all prefigure themes and subjects in Cohen's poetry. And wit as well: compare Klein's "Frigidaire" to Cohen's "The Bus" (*Flowers* 74). And holiness, for in the work of both poets there emerges a reverence for spirituality and belief.

ENGLAND AND GREECE

For his published work, promise, and pronounced support from Layton, Dudek, Scott, and others, Cohen won a two-thousand-dollar Canada Council Arts Scholarship in April 1959 to write a novel in London (Layton won a Senior Canada Council Arts Scholarship as well that spring). Canadian writers then were often overseas: Dorothy Livesay and Mordecai Richler were in London (Richler published *The Apprenticeship of Duddy Kravitz* that year), Mavis Gallant was in Paris, and Margaret Laurence had been in Africa. Layton expresses part of the reason for these exiles in his 1952 preface to his section of *Cerberus*: "The Canadian poet . . . is an exile condemned to live in his own country. He has no public, commands no following, stirs up less interest than last year's license plate" (45). Following Morley Callaghan and John Glassco, who had spent time in Europe in the twenties, and feeling isolated from the European roots of his early life and work, while no doubt finding Montreal and Canada limiting after his exposure to the more adventurous literary world of New York, Cohen seized the opportunity to travel.

At the 24 September 1959 launch of *A Red Carpet for the Sun*, however, Cohen was very visible, although it was Layton who was lionized. Layton entered the Windsor Hotel in Montreal escorted on one side by Aviva and on the other by Cohen, both of whom were necessary to run a kind of interference for him from the mob. That fall Cohen also gave Max Layton, Irving's son, some introductory guitar lessons. Before his departure to England, Cohen joined Layton and Scott in New York for a 12 November reading at the Young Men's / Young Women's Hebrew Association Poetry Center at 92nd Street. Layton received a special four-day visitor's visa because he had been previously barred from entering the United States for political reasons (Cameron, *Irving Layton* 300–01). The successful poetry reading was broadcast on CBC Radio's *Anthology* on 5 March 1960.

London did not provide the excitement and stimulation that Cohen had anticipated. Food, fashion, and the arts seemed uninspired, although he did acquire the "famous blue raincoat," a Burberry, on this trip. He lived with the Pullman family in Hampstead, where Mort Rosengarten had stayed when in London to study sculpture. Mrs. Stella Pullman made Cohen part of the family life, but she insisted that he establish discipline, writing three pages a day. She threatened to evict him should he not make the quota. He began to make friends and for a while saw an English woman named Elizabeth Kenrick. Layton reported to Desmond Pacey in February 1960 that he had had several postcards from Cohen and that he seemed to be thriving. However, the English climate dissatisfied Cohen sooner than Layton was predicting; while depressed and wandering about the city one afternoon in 1960, after he had had a tooth pulled and while suffering from a cold, Cohen discovered Bank Street, in the East End, and noticed the National Bank of Greece. He entered and saw a teller wearing sunglasses, a startling protest against the dreary landscape, as he remarks in *Ladies and Gentlemen . . . Mr. Leonard Cohen*. Asking the man where he had acquired his tan, Cohen learned that it had been in Greece, and he immediately made up his mind that Greece would be his next destination.

Within days, Cohen left for Athens, a city in many ways evocative of Montreal with its linguistic and racial mix, but with a much older and grander history. The city did not charm him for long, however, and he soon decamped for Hydra, which, he had heard, was an artists' colony. Located in the Saronic Gulf just south of the Peloponnesus, and only thirty-five sea miles from Athens, the island is a small, narrow, mountainous rock with little vegetation, having, at that time, approximately two thousand people. In 1821, at the beginning of the Greek War of Independence, in which Byron died, forty thousand people lived there. Hydra had been a magnet for artists since its discovery as an attractive location for movies. *Fodor's* refers to it as "the one place in Greece where there is something like a foreign colony of writers and painters," partly because of the Maison des Artistes established by the Athens School of Fine Arts (271).

Steep flights of steps are the only means of travelling about the town. "The stony path coiled around me / and bound me to night" — from "Hydra 1963" (*Flowers* 65) — describes the port village. Although long favoured for its seclusion and quietness (cars are not permitted; mules provide the only form of transportation), the island possesses only a few poor and stony beaches. Simplicity defined the inexpensive lifestyle that gave Cohen the opportunity to write surrounded by some of the most startling scenery in the Aegean. Music and memories seemed to reoccur as the island exposed its history, art, and religion, three themes that dominate Cohen's later work. The regular rhythm of island life encouraged his writing, and the light provided something "honest and philosophical" Cohen told a journalist in 1963 (qtd. in Ballantyne 2).

Cohen's English girlfriend, Elizabeth, declined to join him in Greece, but on Hydra he soon met the intelligent and attractive Norwegian, Marianne Jensen, then married to Axel Jensen, a novelist. With their infant son, also named Axel, they had sailed to the island. Cohen pursued her to Norway, then intermittently remained with her for the next seven years or so on Hydra. She often appears in photographs with him, most strikingly, perhaps, in the photo used on the rear album jacket of *Songs from a Room* (1969), in which she is typing at Cohen's desk in his Greek house. On the island, Cohen wrote the obligatory three pages a day, prose as well as poetry. In London he had acquired an Olivetti portable typewriter, which now accompanied him on his travels.

In Greece for most of 1960, Cohen continued to work, develop his relationship with Marianne, and keep his contacts with Canada. Colour, heat, and writing dominated his stay, although a new degree of violence and pain began to appear in his poetry illustrated by "Hydra 1960":

Anything that moves is white,
a gull, a wave, a sail,
and moves too purely to be aped.
Smash the pain.

Never pretend peace.
The consolumentum has not,
never will be kissed. Pain
cannot compromise this light. (*Flowers* 54–55)

Cohen spent most of his time on Hydra refining the poems that became his first major success, *The Spice-Box of Earth*. By 27 March 1960, he was able to send to Claire Pratt, an editor at

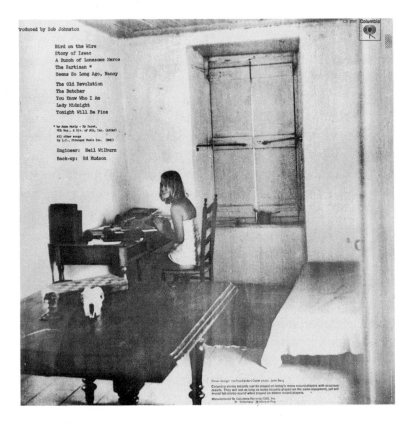

FIGURE 4

Marianne Jensen typing in the bedroom of Cohen's house
in Hydra: the photo appears as the rear album cover of
Songs from a Room *(1969); the skull on the table appears*
in the poem "Hydra 1960" in Flowers for Hitler.

48

McClelland and Stewart, the revised manuscript of the poems, reduced by a third in response to a reader's report. Two important poems remained to be added, he writes in a letter contained in the University of Toronto manuscript collection, but at that stage, he was most interested in the appearance of the book, preferring that the poems not be rendered "in any sort of delicate print. They should be large and black on the page. They should look as though they are meant to be chanted aloud, which is exactly why I wrote them." Heeding his request and deciding to publish a handsome edition, McClelland and Stewart employed the distinguished typographer Frank Newfeld to design the 102-page volume and to contribute line drawings. The limited edition, one of the most impressive books of poetry then published in Canada, sold out in three months.

By November 1960, Cohen was back in Montreal *"to renew my neurotic affiliations"* — as he writes on the back-cover flap of *The Spice-Box of Earth* — and to resume his friendship with Layton and others. Cohen also decided to reapply for the Canada Council grant in December, doing so in one of his few stunts: broke, he borrowed money to hire a limousine with a uniformed driver, sang and smoked marijuana with a friend in the back while cruising to Ottawa, and then "terrorized" the Canada Council staff by chasing them about in a wheelchair, occasionally serenading the secretaries. His unorthodox visit resulted in funding for a return to Hydra in August 1961 to continue writing.

In late fall 1960, Cohen and Layton turned to a new form of writing: collaborative playwriting. In a 1977 interview in *Canadian Theatre Review*, Layton outlined the origin of their dramatic efforts, which began in 1960 (not in 1959, as Layton erroneously recalled), before Cohen departed again for Greece ("Interview" 54). Daily, Layton would visit Cohen at his apartment, and the two would work on what became unpublished plays with the titles "Lights on the Black Water," "A Man Was Killed," "Up with Nothing," and "Enough of Fallen Leaves." Their goal was six plays overall (an additional but unwritten text was to be called "One for the Books," about a communist bookseller). They spent four hours each day, five days a week, yet still had time to write poems or novels. Both hoped to fly to Europe in the spring to work on more plays, Cohen eager — according to Layton — to return to his Norwegian girlfriend.

Having stayed the winter of 1960–61 in Montreal playwriting, Cohen decided to visit Cuba in April, before the release of his second book in May. In Cuba support for Fidel Castro was strong, and people were undergoing a transition from the excesses of the dictator Zaldívar y Batista to a disciplined, no-frills existence under Castro. Into this maelstrom of uncertainty Cohen arrived to explore Havana and the countryside. At one point he was actually surrounded by troops on a beach and then held on suspicion of being part of an American invasion. Layton, nervous about Cohen's visit, wrote to him in mid-April, warning him to leave, thinking that in weeks or days an invasion would begin.

The poorly planned and badly executed Bay of Pigs invasion began on 17 April 1961 and continued for two days: approximately 1,300 men landed; almost 1,200 were captured. Cohen was present during the action that fulfilled the fears of the Cuban people. But he was also there for their triumph against imperialist America; a euphoria swept the country, which may inform the satire in "The Only Tourist in Havana Turns His Thoughts Homeward." The poem encourages Canadian action and self-determination through sarcastic humour:

> let us not take it lying down,
> let us have two Governor Generals
>   at the same time,
> let us have another official language,
> let us determine what it will be,
> let us give a Canada Council Fellowship
>   to the most original suggestion,
> let us teach sex in the home
>   to parents,
> let us threaten to join the U.S.A.
>   and pull out at the last moment. (*Flowers* 38–39)

Borrowing a phrase from Yeats's "The Second Coming," Cohen comically closes with "let us maintain a stony silence / on the St. Lawrence Seaway" (39). Asked why he went to Cuba, he replies that the real reason was his "deep interest in violence." He was obsessed with danger at the time: "I wanted to kill or be killed," he declares with bravado in the documentary *Ladies and Gentlemen . . . Mr. Leonard Cohen.*

Cohen's visit was marked by receipt of Castro's thirteen-page declaration outlining Cuba's creed, which asserts the country's freedom from the imperialism of the United States. Cohen's exposure to the rebellion enhanced his support of personal if not political liberation, but it also showed him the power of the demagogue. "Death of a Leader," also written in Havana and printed in *Flowers for Hitler* (43–45), dramatizes the shattering fall of a politician, while the poem beginning "It is a trust to me," printed in *The Energy of Slaves* (92), records the significance of his discovering trust in another person while in Havana.

By 3 May Cohen was back in Montreal, and the next day he was participating in the Canadian Conference of the Arts at the O'Keefe Centre in Toronto (4–6 May 1961), reading his poetry and Anne Hébert's in French. Layton, however, received the attention with a reading of his new poem, about Jacqueline Kennedy, "Why I Don't Make Love to the First Lady." Claude Bissell, Northrop Frye, and Jean Charles Falardeau opened the conference, followed by Mordecai Richler, Jay Macpherson, Hugh MacLennan, and George Lamming, the West Indian novelist. Robert Weaver, who chaired the poetry reading, was also present. According to Layton, Cohen read beautifully and looked quite "Dorian Grayish."

Reception of *The Spice-Box of Earth*, when it appeared that May, was immediate and admiring, although one comic incident presaged a poor acceptance. Unpacking copies of the book at the McGill Bookstore, a clerk discovered to his shock that they were blind, that is, bound with blank leaves by mistake. Cohen later remarked that had he been there to witness the event, he would not have been able to continue writing poetry (qtd. in Fetherling

38). However, the book became Cohen's first Canadian success, for *Let Us Compare Mythologies* (1956) had appeared only in a limited edition by a small press and was not reprinted until 1966. Viking, Cohen's American publisher, did not release *The Spice-Box of Earth* until 1965, after it had discovered Cohen the novelist. *The Favorite Game* first appeared in London in 1963 and then in New York. In Canada, Cohen was still, presumably, only a poet, for the Canadian edition of *The Favorite Game* was not published until 1970, four years after the publication of *Beautiful Losers*.

On the inside back flap of the dust jacket of *The Spice-Box of Earth* readers discovered the following details about this unknown author:

> Leonard Cohen, 27, McGill graduate, gives his address as Montreal, but as this book was going to press he was enroute to Cuba. He spent last year on the shores of the Aegean Sea, writing as a result of that experience:
>
> *I shouldn't be in Canada at all. Winter is all wrong for me. I belong beside the Mediterranean. My ancestors made a terrible mistake. But I have to keep coming back to Montreal to renew my neurotic affiliations. Greece has the true philosophic climate — you cannot be dishonest in that light. But it's only in Montreal that you can get beat up for wearing a beard. I love Montreal. I hate the speculators who are tearing down my favourite streets and erecting those prisons built in the habit of boredom and gold.*
>
> While he prefers swimming in the Aegean, Leonard Cohen admits a fondness for camping in Northern Quebec. He is currently engaged in writing a novel.

This passage, alternately camp and serious, provides a witty antidote to the serious if youthful portrait of the poet (almost presented as an arty snapshot) on the elegantly designed volume. It emphasizes the exotic and unorthodox, which the collection attempts to promote, while making it clear that Cohen is something special; he may have been born in Montreal, but his life is no longer limited by that city.

The Spice-Box of Earth quickly draws readers into a world of lyrical mystery where metaphysics rather than nature rules. The opening poem, "A Kite Is a Victim," immediately places the reader in a world resonating with meaning, the kite a vehicle connecting one to reaffirming experiences that move in a romantic hierarchy from the self through nature to the heavens, establishing ". . . a contract of glory / that must be made with the sun" (1). The poem also introduces Cohen's use of figurative language through the redefinition of objects in terms of their potential value. Isolating things as poetic images determines their meaning. The second poem, however, "After the Sabbath Prayers," relates this world of significance to a tradition of spirituality that encompasses the physical and everyday as understood through the mystical Hebrew prophet, the Baal Shem Tov. Nature, as a symbol, dominates as a butterfly and the sky, which in the preceding poem are lyrical and pure, become transformed into dual images of beauty and coldness, the ironic consequence of the miracle. The narrator, privileged to see glory, now stands alone but armed in the world:

And how truly great
A miracle this is, that I,
Who this morning saw the Baal Shem's butterfly
Doing its glory in the sun,
Should spend this night in darkness,
Hands pocketed against the flies and cold. (2)

These two works are poems of idealism, unlike much of Cohen's later texts — and the book as a whole celebrates the vision and promise that poetry presents to the world.

Sexuality, however, also emerges as a theme in *The Spice-Box of Earth*, designed not so much to startle as to merge with the mythical and spiritual themes. "Celebration," Cohen's poem about fellatio, expresses this merging clearly through its images of power and history:

When you wrap your tongue
about the amber jewel
and urge my blessing,

I understand those Roman girls
who danced around a shaft of stone
and kissed it till the stone was warm. (60)

But sexuality is also linked to love, identified with nature and
time, as in "As the Mist Leaves No Scar":

As many nights endure
Without a moon or star,
So will we endure
When one is gone and far. (61)

The poems in *The Spice-Box of Earth* are traditional and conservative in structure, creating irony through image and theme,
not through form. A clear example is the sing-song rhythm and
alternating rhyme of the first "Song" (68), although its imagery
is charged with eroticism. It begins:

When with lust I am smitten
To my books I then repair
And read what men have written
Of flesh forbid but fair.

Such stories provide the poet with no rest, and so, in archaic
diction, he casts "down the holy tomes" and lets his eyes wander
". . . to where / The naked girls with silver combs / Are combing
out their hair." And while his subjects continue to sing of beauty,
he must ". . . live with the mortal ring / Of flesh on flesh in dark"
— unsatisfied.

Many of the gentle, lyrical, positive poems in *The Spice-Box of
Earth* remind one of early Yeats in texts such as *The Wind among
the Reeds*, both works containing numerous poems of longing.
Only a few of Cohen's poems break down the poise and restric-

tive verse structures, poems such as "Last Dance at the Four Penny" — about Layton's and Cohen's joyous dancing at the Four Penny Gallery, which transforms a billowing ". . . handkerchief / into a burning cloud" (71) — the expanded haiku for Frank and Marian Scott (76–77), or the wonderful poem for Marc Chagall, "Out of the Land of Heaven" (79–80). Also entering the poems is an important autobiographical element — as in "Priests 1957" — that pointedly criticizes a Judaism that inhibits art and other spiritual ventures: "Must we find all work prosaic / because our grandfather built an early synagogue?" (78).

Characterizing much of the work, however, is the filigree of imagery, as in "Isaiah" (83–85), which displays the remarkable imaginative strength of Cohen the young poet. The cynicism, despair, and alienation that summarize his later poetry are not yet present, but Judaism, love, and the horror of history *do* appear, if only marginally. "The Genius" best embodies these elements: after presenting a litany of possible Jews that the poet might become — ghetto or apostate or banker or Broadway or doctor Jew — he concludes with

For you
I will be a Dachau jew
and lie down in lime
with twisted limbs
and bloated pain
no mind can understand. (87)

This poem, coming near the end of the collection, strongly contradicts the high romanticism of the earlier works, but in doing so it demonstrates Cohen's range of vision and breadth of understanding. But in an effort to turn the reader from the despair of Dachau, Cohen concludes with "Lines from My Grandfather's Journal," which renews a faith in art and the need for articulation, whether of pain or pleasure. "It is strange," writes the narrator/grandfather, but not surprising "that even now," in the midst of remembering the suffering of Jews and others, "prayer is my natural language . . ." (89). In the end, there is still hope because "The real deserts are outside of tradition . . ." (92). This poem, which mixes prose and verse, promises future richness, which the spice-box itself, cited on the last page, contains and which the final, prayer-like invocation sustains:

Lead your priest
from grave to vineyard.
Lay him down
where air is sweet. (94)

By August 1961 Cohen was back in Greece — where his "Gothic insincerities were purged" and his "style purified under the influence of empty mountains and a foreign mate who cherished simple English," as he writes in a 1963 press release from Viking. He wrote to Layton late in August that he had seen corpses in the sea and witnessed " 'assassins' drugs.' From which I gather the Greek wines are too strong for him," Layton explains to Desmond Pacey in a letter dated 28 August 1961. Cohen returned to a small but cherished house in Hydra, which he had purchased for $1,500 and which he described in October in a letter to his sister Esther. He typed the letter at a solid, square table in the kitchen, with three kerosene lamps providing light. "The House," a poem composed on 4 July 1963 and published in *Flowers for Hitler* (85), similarly praises his life-centred home in Hydra. Greece, however, plays a surprisingly small part in his writing as subject or setting. Hydra was a retreat, an alternative to life in Montreal or New York with his publishers, friends, and obligations. Although it was the centre of Cohen's private life, Greece has only a minor presence in his poetry and song and none in his fiction.

Cohen returned to Hydra satisfied with his poetic but not novelistic success. An annuity of $750 supplemented his second Canada Council Arts Scholarship, which he won in 1960. On the island, Cohen became good friends with Australian writers

George Johnston and his wife Charmaine Clift, both novelists, while other writers such as Allen Ginsberg and Gregory Corso passed through. Increasingly, political issues held Cohen's interest, as reflected in various poems and letters.

FAVOURITE GAMES

In addition to writing and revising his poetry, Cohen continued to compose his first published novel throughout 1961 and 1962, restructuring and retitling the text, initially entitled "Beauty at Close Quarters: An Anthology." A preliminary reader's report of January 1962 praises the beauty of the writing but also notes that "some of the book is either obscene or near obscene — that is, in the conventionally accepted sense." The novel could be better shaped but "is redeemed from being merely erotic by the carefully drawn background and the Jewish philosophy of life. . . . [But] the title is terrible, vulgar and out of keeping with the style of the novel." Two words, however, tellingly conclude the report: "very saleable."

Secker in London accepted the manuscript, publishing the book in October 1963; Viking Press in New York did not receive corrected galleys until May, and publication did not occur until September. Differences between British and American spelling are apparent (*The Favourite Game* is the spelling of the British edition). The British text and the Canadian offset paperback edition of 1970, the book's first appearance in Canada, print the complete text of Cohen's poem "As the Mist Leaves No Scar," from *The Spice-Box of Earth*, after the dedication "To my mother." The American edition has no epigraph, and the dedication is truncated to read, "TO ———, AS PROMISED," thereby making it more mystifying and obscure. The novel has been translated into Swedish, French, Danish, German, Spanish, and Italian.

The *New York Times* headlines its account of the book "Young Bohemians — Canadian Style," and the reviewer, Charles Poore, calls the work a "churningly avant-garde novel." Other reviewers were equally unsympathetic, criticizing the laboured writing and the lengthy if not tedious autobiographical focus on adolescence and sexual discovery. Nevertheless, the dust-jacket blurb — "where the 'favourite game' is love" — on the New Canadian Library reprint was later repeatedly cited. Yet some reviewers acknowledged the writing as showing talent and promise.

A sixties "portrait of the artist as a young man," *The Favorite Game* nevertheless differs from other *kunstlerroman* (novels about the growth of young artists, James Joyce's *A Portrait of the Artist as a Young Man* or Thomas Mann's *Doktor Faustus*, for instance) by its Montreal setting and Canadian details. In his efforts to be the Keats of Canada, the hero, Lawrence Breavman, feels that Canadians are eager for the "mild Dylan Thomas, talent and behavior modified for Canadian tastes" (110). The hero's name, and the setting in the last quarter of the novel, draw on Cohen's summer adventures at Pripstein's Camp, where the son-in-law of the owner, named Braverman, was a likely source for Cohen's hero, Breavman. With its romantic form and its content about the artist discovering his vocation, the novel is important for an understanding of Cohen's developing life and work — it charts his break with the world of Westmount and his need to create, and it portrays a stage in his evolving voice and the subject matter of his poetry and subsequent novel, *Beautiful Losers*. It also focuses on sexual awakening, thus anticipating a primary focus in his next novel. And in both texts, the flesh is made word, ironically reversing the homily.

Scars, movies, photographs, and sex are among the dominant images in *The Favorite Game*, acting also as guides to the reliance on various texts in the book. The epigraph, "As the Mist Leaves No Scar," introduces ironic references to scars, which reappear on the first page; film citations begin on page five, manifesting distortion as well as a record: "Breavman is mutilating the film in his efforts at history." His action is necessary, however, in order for him to deal with the past, for the death of his father, which opens the book, must be confronted and processed. The re-creation or rewriting of history, and through that act its assessment, become principal activities for the hero. Krantz, Breavman's sidekick (akin to F. in *Beautiful Losers*) — Martin is another — is the foil to the hero's growth. Yet what drives Breavman to become an artist has as much to do with power as it does with creativity. His words can overpower and leave scars, as he explains to Tamara: "I want to touch people like a magician, to change them or hurt them, leave my brand, make them beautiful" (106–07). The link between pain and beauty is clear and reflective of the constant exchange between the two in Cohen's work.

The theme of self-defeat, however, also present in Cohen's poetry, finds confirmation in Breavman's failure to control Shell's beauty: "The loveliness she composed seemed to rebel and escape her, as sometimes a poem under the pen becomes wild and uncontrollable" (171). Breavman cannot forgive himself for this impotence, which he attempts to overcome by writing, although, ironically, he does not "realize that Shell was won not by the text but by the totality of his attention" (179). For the sake of his art and his need to create beauty, however, he leaves Shell, as he has left Bertha and Tamara, a proleptic act for Cohen himself, who has found it difficult to stay with women because of their apparent entrapment of his imagination, as he dramatizes in "My Life in Art." Breavman summarizes this paradox in "Poems of parting a man writes to a woman he will not let out of his sight" (185). This statement exposes a central conflict in all of Cohen's work: his art demands distancing from the very sources that feed it. His seeming indifference to the women in his texts originates in his focus on creativity, generated initially by sexual desire and acceptance. But only if he leaves these women can he write.

Movies in *The Favorite Game* similarly function to restore and then destroy the past, anticipating the role of history in *Beautiful Losers*. Rather than being linear or historical records, the home movies, documentaries, and pornographic films (for example, "Thirty Ways to Screw," designed to revitalize the tedious marriages of the country, Breavman adds [26]) are recurrent encounters with the past that enclose rather than expand the life of the subject — as Cohen himself possibly thought at the time about the seemingly endless home movies that his father had taken. In order to liberate the present by breaking down the past, they must be mutilated.

The voyeuristic element of film creates Breavman's later self-dramatization as an actor: "He was in a film and the machine was whirring into slower and slower motion" (72). Often, he sees himself performing, as with Norma (75), and there always seems to be a slow-motion movie about him running through his mind. However, like the magician and the hypnotist, two constant references for Breavman, the artist wants to control, as Krantz seems to do in Breavman's vision of him blending photographic images: he "seemed to be cutting into the natural progression of time, like a movie frozen into a single image and then released to run again" (104).

A self-conscious development of the theme of creation and the conditions necessary for it is the principal accomplishment of *The Favorite Game*, which stands as something of an artistic manifesto for Cohen. Consistent with various poems are the views that "Deprivation is the mother of poetry" (26) and that nothing equals the pleasure of self-creation. Indeed, the only kind of sexual love that matters is "the love of the creator for his creation. In other words, the love of the creator for himself" (95). Contentment risks the loss of creation, even though "A scar is what happens when the word is made flesh" (3). Blackening his pages (177), a phrase that Cohen repeatedly uses to describe his work, is Breavman's response to the challenge of Stéphane Mallarmé's white page. But such blackening is also a scarring and branding — for art begins only when love ends. And the favourite game is not love but the impression in the snow, the trace of the presence of an individual or experience left through art or possibly memory.

Cohen spent the summer of 1963 trying to place portions of *The Favorite Game* in magazines and to sell various short stories, mostly without success. These efforts were part of his plan to find a wider audience in magazines that people *did* read, rather than limiting his readership to the small-circulation, highbrowed little magazines. *Playboy* quickly rejected a portion of the novel, but *Cavalier* took a section for $750 American. Encouraged, Cohen wrote to his New York agent, Marian McNamara, that *The Favorite Game* could easily become a movie and should be shopped around. Little came of the effort, however. By October 1963, Cohen was again in Montreal to celebrate the appearance of *The Favorite Game* in New York the previous month and to accept the five-hundred-dollar first prize in a cbc competition for new Canadian poets. His cocelebrant was Layton, who told Pacey that after the celebration he and Cohen had planned to raid city hall and write poems on all the files they could find (letter).

While in and out of the Montreal scene during the winter of 1963, Cohen met a dancer, Suzanne Verdal, one of several female inspirations for two poems in *Parasites of Heaven* beginning "Suzanne wears a leather coat" and (the better known of the two) "Suzanne takes you down" (31, 70). The first provides a powerful image of this dangerous woman who ". . . won't stop / to bandage the fractures she walks between"; and while she disrupts the city with her beauty, no one can ". . . build the ant-full crystal city / she would splinter with the tone of her step." The second poem, recorded as "Suzanne," the first song on Cohen's first album, *Songs of Leonard Cohen* (1968), has become his best known but least literary piece. The song was mostly written but lacked focus until Suzanne Vaillancourt, a professional dancer and the wife of Montreal sculptor Armand Vaillancourt, took Cohen to her place, something like a loft, near the river in St. Marks. A number of images then came together for Cohen, including the sailor's church. The second verse, beginning "Jesus was a sailor," reflects Cohen's sense of Montreal as a holy city.

With the surrealist imagery, theme of the femme fatale, and mixture of religion and rebirth, the poem, written in 1963, and

FIGURE 5

Cohen, the young first-novelist, in a posed shot in October 1963.

the song, recorded in 1966, captured the tone of the sixties, mixing a gentle hedonism with an appeal to a hippie lifestyle. An interesting variation between the poem and the song are the last lines, however. In *Parasites of Heaven* (71) and *Selected Poems 1956–1968* (209–10), they read, "and you're sure that she can find you / because she's touched her perfect body / with her mind." In the song the line reads, "And you know that you can trust her / For she's touched your perfect body with her mind," thus shifting the sense and altering the state of the outsider. About this line Cohen remarked that, because Suzanne was the wife of a friend, he couldn't touch her with anything but his mind. Liner notes for *The Best of Leonard Cohen* recount the episode, although in less detail, adding that "her hospitality was immaculate. . . . The publishing rights were lost in New York City but it is probably appropriate that I don't own this song. Just the other day I heard some people singing it on a ship in the Caspian Sea."

Cohen stayed in Montreal through the winter of 1963–64 considering various projects, including the English soundtrack for Claude Jutra's film, *A tout prendre*, which had won first prize at the Montreal Film Festival in 1962. In 1963 Cohen worked on the English subtitles for the movie, a film dealing with an illicit affair between a young Montrealer and a Negro fashion model. At the Montreal première, an underdressed Layton, his wife Aviva, and his friend Roy MacSkimming arrived at the theatre with their engraved invitation to find a gala Québécois cultural event with Cohen bedecked in tails, cape, and silver-topped cane surrounded by half a dozen stunning women. Layton called across the lobby, "Leonard, you rascal! What's up? Who are your friends?" Cohen frowned and hissed, "Shhh, Irving, — speak *French*." "But Leonard," Irving boomed, "I don't *speak* French!" (qtd. in MacSkimming, "Importance" 18).

Late October 1964 saw the publication of *Flowers for Hitler*, a controversial and for some a disappointing book that contains many of Cohen's poems about Greece and European history. Erotica and guilt emerge as startling themes, causing Al Purdy to (over)state that "there has never been a book like *Flowers for*

Hitler published in Canada'' (14). Cohen wrote a number of the poems on a ship that took a month to travel from Oslo, which Cohen had left on 16 May 1962, to Patras in the Peloponnesus.

On the back cover of the book, Cohen provides a summary of his work:

> This book moves me from the world of the golden-boy poet into the dung pile of the front-line writer. I didn't plan it this way. I loved the tender notices *Spice-Box* got but they embarrassed me a little. *Hitler* won't get the same hospitality from the papers. My sounds are too new, therefore people will say: this is derivative, this is slight, his power has failed. Well, I say that there has never been a book like this, prose or poetry, written in Canada. All I ask is that you put it in the hands of my generation and it will be recognized.

Cohen had cabled Jack McClelland to suppress this summary, and its publication upset him: it "has made me and the book a hell of a lot of enemies. It was very important that a Jew's book on Hitler be free from arrogant personal promotion," he later wrote to McClelland (qtd. in Ondaatje 62n1), who replied that the appearance of the blurb did not harm sales. Production of the book was marked by acrimonious debate, beginning with disagreements over the value of the poetry. Cohen responded vitriolically to the original design of the book, the publisher apparently planning a cover with a picture of a woman's body and Cohen's face for her breasts (Ondaatje 62n1).

However, the inflated prose of the blurb (which appeared only on the original edition and not on the reissues; also dropped was Frank Newfeld's cover drawing) was partially correct. Many reviewers did complain that the poems were derivative and that the energy of *The Spice-Box of Earth* had dissipated. Critics complained about the absence of a new style and Cohen's failure to generate a revolution in prosody, although the work does include several prose poems, a poem with annotations ("The Pure List and the Commentary"), illustrations, and a drama, "The New Step." In "A NOTE ON THE TITLE," Cohen writes that

A
while ago
this book would
have been called
SUNSHINE FOR NAPOLEON,
and earlier still it
would have been
called
WALLS FOR GENGHIS KHAN. ([iii])

The focus on collective guilt and the burden of modern history, however, mark the weightiness of the collection. In part these themes may be a response to Layton's question in *Balls for a One-Armed Juggler*, published the year before: "Where is the poet who can make clear for us Belsen?" (xviii). Cohen's answer is partly found in an exchange with Eli Mandel, who noted that the concentration camp is an obsessive image for Cohen. When asked why, Cohen replies, "Well, cos I wish they'd let me out" (qtd. in Ondaatje 35). Hitler, Goebbels, Göring, Eichmann, and Castro appear in Cohen's text, along with sex and drugs. Partially hidden in his earlier work, these figures of evil and repression now orient the poet's experience, as in "The Drawer's Condition on November 28, 1961" or in "Indictment of the Blue Hole," dated 28 January 1962. The Holocaust is present, although as early as "Lovers," in *Let Us Compare Mythologies*, Cohen was confronting the reality and pain of this historical event. But it becomes ironic in "On Hearing a Name Long Unspoken":

History is a needle
for putting men asleep
anointed with the poison
of all they want to keep. (*Flowers* 25)

Nevertheless, it must be opposed through the horrifically ironic realization in "It Uses Us!" that *"All things can be done* / whisper museum ovens of / a war that Freedom won" (31). Here, the satire of A.M. Klein's *The Hitleriad* becomes the biting irony of a world that has still not awakened to the tragedy of the Holocaust.

Supplementing history in the book is Montreal. A number of the poems refer to the political and social changes in the city and how they foreshadow a shift in the future of Canada while confirming the inhibiting dimension of the culture: in "Montreal 1964," the poet laments that ". . . my absolute poems will be crumpled / under a marble asylum / my absolute flight snarled like old fishing line" (35). But uniting the diverse poems, in addition to an element of surrealism in many, as in "The Lists," is the sense that history is important — if one can remember it (see "A Migrating Dialogue") — and that "Faces must be forged under the hammer / of savage ideas," as in "Cherry Orchards" (122). As Kerensky wanders in Montreal, Cohen walks the harbour of Hydra, and his mother laughs in her old Cadillac, while the stars in "Another Night with Telescope"

> . . . wait for no man's discipline
>   but as they wheel
> from sky to sky they rake
>   our lives with pins of light. (128)

Although the judgement of *Flowers for Hitler* has been mixed, some contemporaries noted the uncompromising character of the work and its deeper range. Milton Wilson declares that ". . . Cohen is potentially the most important writer that Canadian poetry has produced since 1950 — not merely the most talented, but also . . . the most professionally committed to making the most of his talent" (353). The country was beginning to take note of its absent poet.

But absence from Canada did not define Cohen in the fall of 1964: in October he won the four-thousand-dollar first prize in the English-language competition for the Prix littéraire du Québec for *The Favorite Game*, and that fall he participated in a reading tour with Layton, Birney, and Gotlieb, engineered by Jack

McClelland and filmed by the National Film Board. It was a good year for Cohen: he earned seventeen thousand dollars. The tour contrasted Layton's outrageous and flirtatious image with Cohen's hard and dark image. *Time* describes Cohen at the University of Western Ontario dressed in a leather jacket and playing it cool before the appreciative audience ("Poets' Progress"). The hipster Cohen, so called by Don Owen, the NFB director, dominates the documentary film, appropriately entitled *Ladies and Gentlemen . . . Mr. Leonard Cohen.*

This film, originally to be an account of all four poets, was edited to deal exclusively with the most fascinating of the group. It is also the first of several films made about and with Cohen: *The Song of Leonard Cohen*, by Harry Rasky (1980, CBC), and *I Am a Hotel*, by Allan Nichols (1983, CTV), are two of the better known ones. The 1965 film, which Donald Brittain scripted and codirected with Owen, begins with Cohen delivering a comic monologue about his visit to a friend in a Montreal mental hospital. A series of readings and voice-overs then accompanies a variety of images of Cohen in Montreal as a child, as an adult, in a hotel room, in Ben's Delicatessen, and in the street. But the film also suggests, even at this early stage in his career, Cohen's sense of vulnerability and humbleness before the responsibility of his vision, which later works, especially *Book of Mercy*, elaborate.

A press conference with Cohen and Layton, presided over by Pierre Berton, forms part of the film. Provoked by the journalists, Cohen defines the "state of grace" that he seeks: it is "the kind of balance with which you rise to the chaos you find around you. It's not a matter of resolving the chaos, because there's something arrogant and war-like about putting the world to order." A discussion with friends on the *I Ching* and comments on his experiment with vegetarianism follow, extended by remarks on the value of photography and of being photographed as Cohen watches part of the film in a studio. Sexuality and its importance, plus a critique of academics and their pretensions, are also present. The film ends reflexively, as Cohen

FIGURE 6

*Cohen, Irving Layton, Phyllis Gotlieb, and Earle Birney, the four
poets whose reading tour in the fall of 1964 Donald Brittain filmed
for the National Film Board: in final form the film was released
as* Ladies and Gentlemen . . . Mr. Leonard Cohen.

But the book is also a historical work, with roots in the pictures of Catherine Tekakwitha that Cohen saw in the apartment of his friend Alanis Obamsawin, an Abenaquis Native ("Leonard Cohen: The Poet" 29). Obamsawin lent Cohen a rare book on Tekakwitha that he took with him in Greece, P. Edouard Lecompte's *Une vierge iroquoise: Catherine Tekakwitha, le lis de bords de la Mohawk et du St.-Laurent (1656–1680)* (1927). (It was translated by Sister Francis, or Isabel Hamilton Melick, in 1932 as *An Iroquois Virgin: Catherine Tekakwitha, Lily of the Mohawk and the St. Lawrence, 1656–1680*.) A volume entitled *Jesuits in North America* and an authorized biography of Catherine supplemented the French text and enlarged his presentation of the first Native saint. A 1943 American comic book entitled *Blue Beetle*, in which an early version of Spider Man — in a blue outfit and possessing the magical powers of ancient Egypt through an azure scarab worn on his belt — combats evil, also contributed to the visual imaginativeness Cohen presents. The comic book is incorporated into the novel as the source of an ad for a bodybuilding scheme and cited with *Captain Marvel* and *Plastic Man* (116). As F. comments in the novel, "the texts had got to me" (169), critically summarizing Cohen's placement of works within his work. Cohen remarked that "radio was the mythology of my childhood" and that he wrote the novel beside a radio, "the only other human voice in the room." He also claimed that a farmer's almanac and Longfellow's *The Song of Hiawatha* were source books for him (Ondaatje 62n1).

To a journalist in France, Cohen explained that writing the novel was almost a test of character, saying that 1965 was a bad year for him: "I hated myself. I said if I couldn't even write, it wasn't worth living. So I sat down to my desk and said I would use only the books that were there: a rare book on Catherine Tekakwitha . . . , a 1943 Blue Beetle comic book and a few others." The book "was written with blood," he explained: "at the end I was writing 20 hours a day and going only on pep drugs and hashish" (qtd. in Lumsden 72). The copy on the jacket flap, possibly written by Cohen, best describes the novel:

Beautiful Losers is a love story, a psalm, a Black Mass, a monument, a satire, a prayer, a shriek, a road map through the wilderness, a joke, a tasteless affront, an hallucination, a bore, an irrelevant display of diseased virtuosity, a Jesuitical tract, an Orange sneer, a scatological Lutheran extravagance — in short a disagreeable religious epic of incomparable beauty.

Intertextuality and intratextuality define the novel, a palimpsest of Canadian history and politics extending the theme of historical oppression that MacLennan articulates in *Two Solitudes*. In *Beautiful Losers*, what the British imposed on the French, the Jesuit missionaries impose on the Iroquois, and English Canada imposes on contemporary Quebec in the sixties of the novel. Set in 1917, the opening of MacLennan's novel anticipates these levels of oppression: it focuses on the imposition of conscription by the English on the French, thereby "trying to force their conquest on Quebec a second time," as Father Beaubien understands it. He then questions the possibility of the French-Canadian commitment to Canada:

How could French-Canadians — the only real Canadians — feel loyalty to a people who had conquered and humiliated them. . . . [But] France herself was no better; she had deserted her Canadians a century and a half ago, had left them in the snow and ice along the Saint Lawrence surrounded by their enemies, had later murdered her anointed king and then turned atheist. (7)

Exploring this subject through the radical form of *Beautiful Losers*, Cohen extends awareness of a Canadian problem that is too often hidden: political repression.

F. is guru to the unnamed, folklorist-anthropologist-cum-narrator. A member of Parliament and a capitalist, F. is also a revolutionary and Mephistophelian character who leads the narrator and Edith down various false and dangerous paths in a sometimes perverse search for modern sainthood, to be achieved by inversion. His Nietzschean character finds confirmation in *Twilight of the Idols*, Nietzsche's late work, which Cohen quotes through several statements by F.

To the question "What is a saint?", F. answers:

A saint is someone who has achieved a remote human possibility. It is impossible to say what that possibility is. I think it has something to do with the energy of love. Contact with this energy results in the exercise of a kind of balance in the chaos of existence. A saint does not dissolve the chaos; if he did the world would have changed long ago. . . . It is a kind of balance that is his glory. He rides the drifts like an escaped ski. (95)

The first part of the novel is about F.'s attempts to get the narrator to recover such emotions. A central episode, which blends the erotic with the political and the emotional, occurs when they are drawn to a demonstration against the visit of Queen Elizabeth to Montreal in 1964. They join an agitated crowd that shouts, "Give us back our History! The English have stolen our History!" (118), and hear the cries of a French-Canadian filmmaker from the NFB: "History decrees that there are Losers and Winners. History cares nothing for cases, History cares only whose Turn it is" (119). Stimulated by a female hand thrust in his pants, the narrator suddenly cries out in support of the separatists, becoming more agitated as the crowd disperses. But suddenly recognized as an English-speaking Jew, he is threatened. Rescued by F. before the crowd attacks him, the narrator, like the crowd, becomes impotent, his sexual desire unconsummated. Interestingly, it is the filmmaker in the scene who provides the images of identity needed to shape the nationalist agenda. This scene anticipates the October revolution of 1970, during which the Front de libération de Québec (FLQ) cell kidnapped James Cross, finding its inspiration in the semi-documentary film, *The Battle of Algiers*. For the revolutionaries, film replaces book; or, as F. remarks, "I wanted to show Brigitte Bardot around revolutionary Montréal" (205).

Balancing the new French Canada and forging a new future is "the New Jew," defined in a long letter from F. to the narrator:

> Who is the New Jew?
>
> The New Jew loses his mind gracefully. He applies finance to abstraction resulting in successful messianic politics, colorful showers of meteorites and other symbolic weather. He has induced amnesia by a repetitious study of history, his very forgetfulness caressed by facts which he accepts with visible enthusiasm. . . . The New Jew is the founder of Magic Canada, Magic French Québec, and Magic America. He demonstrates that yearning brings surprises. (160–61)

This passage ironically prefigures the betrayal of Jewish sympathy for the Québécois while claiming that the spirit of the Jew as wanderer and victim is the spirit that founds nations. Only Jews, F. suggests, possess a messianic sense of history. But as he claims near the end of his letter, in his quest for an independent Quebec, "I want to hammer a beautiful colored bruise on the whole American monolith. . . . I want History to jump on Canada's spine with sharp skates" (186–87).

To convey the multiplicity of ideas in the novel, Cohen uses a multiplicity of forms: letters, journals, historical narrative, grammar books, instructions,ons cinematic flashes, drama, advertisements, self-conscious interruptions, footnotes, lists, catalogues, poetry. This approach fulfils his claim that "I am going to show you everything *happening*" (164). Various languages — Greek, Latin, French, English, and Iroquois (three of them neatly coming together on page 216 in one paragraph) — also appear. And near the end of the novel, the narrator can say, ". . . I have shown you *how it happens*, from style to style, from kiss to kiss" (182). Such bursting, encyclopaedic energy exceeds the limits of its forms, forcing the narrator to interrupt with, "O Reader, do you know that a man is writing this? A man like you . . ." (102).

The System Theatre, as both the location for the remarkable movies that are witnessed and the scene of the frenzied eroticism of the telephone dance, is the metaphor of this creative process. In this world of shadows, the cinema becomes reality and therefore essential: ". . . I've got to get to a movie . . . , a movie will put me back in my skin . . ." says the narrator at one point (64). Yet the system — whether theatre, language, or even thought — breaks down at the end through the surreal, inverted world of the text, in which even inanimate objects, such as "the Danish Vibrator," which rumbles out of the hotel room and down the beach out to sea (180), or the radio, transpose themselves into what they desire: "(CLOSE-UP OF RADIO EXHIBITING A MOTION PICTURE OF ITSELF)" (226). Deconstructing the illusion becomes a literal exercise at the end when, in the movie theatre, the narrator synchronizes his blinking eyes with the shutter of the projector. The screen goes black, the movie is invisible, and some in the audience realize they are "in the presence of a Master of the Yoga of the Movie Position" (236). Not suspense but blankness occurs, establishing a purity of vision. It is the achievement, if only for a moment, of "the Clear Light" that, if one cannot dwell in it, nonetheless forces one to "deal with symbols" (185). Dissolve at the end into a movie of Ray Charles, whose singing of "Ol' Man River" provides the epigraph to the book, "Somebody said lift that bale."

"I had an idea of what a man should look like, but it kept changing," the narrator remarks (175), and his comment is aptly suited to understanding the metamorphosis of character and text in this powerful, disturbing, ultimately challenging work, which fulfils its early declaration: "Desire changes the world!" (5). Through the politics of slavery and servitude, through the double vision of the present and the past, through the lives of Edith and Catherine, F. and the narrator, the reader is brought to face a world of devastating yet mesmerizing energy. A twelve-day fast marked Cohen's completion of the work, necessary for him to recover from the nihilistic experience of writing himself out and establishing the purity of language, appropriately expressed in the novel through shadows. The narrator's goal is to cast a shadow, emptying himself so that he can receive what is newly achieved. But language, a transparent medium, also becomes a vehicle used to glimpse the sacred: "God is alive. Magic is afoot" (157).

Not surprisingly, condemnation and celebration greeted a novel, especially a Canadian novel, stressing sainthood through sexuality. Some reviewers quickly labelled *Beautiful Losers* obscene; others compared it to Pynchon, John Barth, or Burroughs. The *Maclean's* headline for its 1 October 1966 story on Cohen dramatized public misgivings by asking, "Is the World (or Anybody) Ready for Leonard Cohen?" (18), while the photo caption refers to him as "a sort of Jewish Byron" (19). In the article, he stresses that "Nobody writes who doesn't really drive himself" (qtd. in Ruddy 34). But critics' hesitancy contrasts with the response of writers to the novel; bill bissett says it clearly in *Alphabet*: "i give th book of Cohens a good review, a great review, easily millions stars" (94). Despite the Canadian uncertainty in responding to *Beautiful Losers*, a Montreal TV station offered Cohen a position as host; he declined.

"All my arabesques are for publication," writes the narrator in *Beautiful Losers* (151–52), and *Parasites of Heaven*, also published in 1966, confirms this excess. An uneven, inclusive collection, it reflects the least rigour and selectivity by Cohen. Several of the poems date from 1957 and 1958, suggesting that he reached into the past to fill out the book. Many of them appear as sketches for songs, several of which — notably "Suzanne," "The Master Song," "Teachers," and "Avalanche" — are better known as recordings. Thematic coherence seems to be absent, and the only formal experiment is a number of short prose poems that are analogous to sections of *Beautiful Losers* but without the dramatic development and context of the novel. Nevertheless, they continue the themes of spirituality and prepare readers for Cohen's later involvement with a series of sacred texts. The prose poem that begins "In the Bible generations pass in a paragraph . . ." is representative. In this account of biblical compression

FIGURE 7

Cohen and Marianne Jensen in Montreal in 1966, the year
Beautiful Losers *and* Parasites of Heaven *were published.*

(and confusion) — "the creation of the world consumes a page" — the narrator admits that he can never tell one important dynasty from another and that he cannot clearly separate the valuable from the worthless, preferring to include all (16). Response to the holy text overall rather than to individual details is what is crucial, but in this poem and in others, such as that beginning "Here we are at the window" (23), one experiences powerful metaphysical prose that is equally innocent and knowledgeable.

Also appearing in the collection is the antipoem, a work that relies on factual, prosaic statements, as in the poem that begins "Snow is falling" (53), written in 1958. This stance presages that developed in *The Energy of Slaves* (1972), in which the function of poetry is antithetical to any aesthetic but destruction. In *Parasites of Heaven*, the subjective self dominates; the historical and social arenas are eliminated. Where *Flowers for Hitler* shows a social and moral awareness of its age, *Parasites of Heaven* focuses on the self — "You said you wanted me naked so I hung my skin in the wind" (50) — and, occasionally, on the banal, as in the poem beginning "He was lame" (46). Yet, while Cohen can declare that "Poetry is no substitute for survival" (61), he still requires a certain humiliation in order to create:

Network of created fire,
maim my love and my desire.
Make me poor so I may be
servant in the world I see. (63)

Running throughout is the self-consciousness of double vision, stated clearly in the poem beginning "He was beautiful when he sat alone, he was like me . . ." (66), and in the self-reflexive remark on the nature of the text at the end: "It is not a question mark, it is not an exclamation point, it is a full stop by the man who wrote Parasites of Heaven" (67). The understated tone of these poems is characteristic, driven by Cohen's humility before the grandeur of the pain and vision, and summarized at this midpoint in his career by the poem beginning "I've seen some lonely history"; it concludes:

I'm standing here before you
I don't know what I bring
If you can hear the music
Why don't you help me sing. (59)

The appearance of *Parasites of Heaven* following *Beautiful Losers* marks the apogee of Cohen's literary notoriety — to be exceeded only by the success of *Selected Poems 1956–1968* (1968). Although Cohen had sought to extend the shock and originality of *Flowers for Hitler*, *Parasites of Heaven*, while sustaining many of the same themes and much of the tone of his earlier work, lacks its care and precision of language. Nonetheless, it ensured Cohen's presence not only in Canada but also elsewhere. Dedicated to Layton, the work surveys the by-then-expected key of despair, as expressed in "I was walking on a tightrope / That was buried in the mud" (59).

In 1966 Dudek edited an important anthology for Macmillan, *Poetry of Our Time: An Introduction to Twentieth-Century Poetry Including Modern Canadian Poetry*. He refers to Cohen (and poets like him) as being "beyond classification" (198); nevertheless, "his lyrical nerve, his spontaneous frankness, [and his] engaging personality" had established his remarkable reputation. "He belongs," Dudek concludes, "to the new generation which includes the beats, the Beatles, and the *boîtes à chanson*" (281). Uniting the avant-garde with pop stars and French café singers was apt, for Cohen was becoming a figure difficult to categorize yet immensely appealing.

SINGER/PROPHET

Rather than consolidating his literary reputation after *Beautiful Losers* and *Parasites of Heaven*, Cohen altered his career by shifting almost exclusively to music. Having written and performed from his teenage years, he was determined to reach a larger audience — and with the help and popularity of musicians such as Bob

Dylan and Judy Collins, and the willingness of record companies to capitalize on the unexplored market for electronic folk music driven by a rock-and-roll beat, he succeeded. He also realized that his books, which had largely been critical successes, had made him very little money.

Dylan literally caused a resurgence of folk rock in the sixties with his electrifying performance of "Like a Rolling Stone" at the 1965 Newport Folk Festival. The fusion of rock-and-roll music with thoughtful folk lyrics on his album *Bringing It All Back Home*, also released in 1965, thrust him into the national spotlight. His popular success, based on his substantial lyrics, inspired other writers/singers to combine singing with substance — from Neil Young to Lou Reed and Jim Morrison. The timing of this shift enhanced the acceptance of Cohen as a singer/poet, beginning in 1966 when Collins recorded "Suzanne."

Intending to go to Nashville to become a country-and-western singer and absorb the musical culture there, Cohen, as he has often repeated, was "hijacked" by New York. In 1966, with a loan from his old Montreal friend Robert Hershorn (a successful clothing manufacturer who later died in Hong Kong under suspicious circumstances), Cohen was able to settle for a while on the sixth floor of the Chelsea Hotel on 23rd Street, the home of numerous artists, writers, and musicians. During his stay, no less than Joan Baez, Bob Dylan, Jimi Hendrix, and Janis Joplin visited the well-known bohemian address. Previous residents included William S. Burroughs, Virgil Thomson, Thomas Wolfe, and Arthur Miller, who called it "a ceaseless party" (qtd. in Dorman 176). Dylan Thomas drank himself to death in room 206; Sid Vicious would murder his girlfriend Nancy Spungeon there.

Cohen lived in a small, cupboard-sized room mostly taken up by two single beds and his guitar. "Chelsea Hotel #2," recorded on *New Skin for the Old Ceremony* (1974), narrates the unhappy experiences and early death of Janis Joplin, with whom Cohen had a brief affair at the Chelsea. He even finds macabre humour in his romantic success:

You told me once
again you preferred
handsome men, but for
me you would make an
exception.

At the close of the song, a mood of resignation reigns over his
forgotten love:

I don't mean to
suggest that I loved you the best; I don't keep track of each
fallen robin.
I remember you well
in the Chelsea Hotel —
that's all, I don't even
think of you that often.

Through the Montreal-born agent Mary Martin, an assistant
to Albert Grossman (Dylan's manager), Cohen met Judy Collins
and sang several of his compositions in her living room. She liked
none of them but encouraged him to call if he had any other
songs. He later sang "Suzanne" to her over the phone from
Montreal, and she quickly recorded it for her 1966 release *In My
Life*. Her next album, *Wildflowers* (1967), contains "Sisters of
Mercy," "Priests," and "Hey, That's No Way to Say Goodbye,"
plus her own hit, "Both Sides Now." It became her best-selling
album, reaching number five and remaining on the charts for
seventy-five weeks. In October 1967, a single of "Suzanne" by
the actor Noel Harrison hit number fifty-six on the national
singles list.

John Hammond, the artists-and-repertory man at Columbia
who had discovered Billie Holiday, nurtured Count Basie, signed
Bob Dylan, and later worked with Bruce Springsteen, heard
Cohen's song on a prerelease tape of Collins's *In My Life* and
quickly sought to sign him, the idea being that if a singer such
as Dylan could win acclaim as a poet, then a poet such as Cohen

might establish a following as a singer. The signing was in September 1966, after Hammond had also viewed *Ladies and Gentlemen . . . Mr. Leonard Cohen* at the CBC offices in New York.

Collins at this time was introducing Cohen to many key musicians and artists in New York, including Dylan, Reed, Andy Warhol, and The Velvet Underground, with the pop-art icon, Nico, with whom Cohen was soon infatuated. His plan at this time "was to make a record, make some money, and go back to writing books. I had no idea I'd end up in hotel rooms for the rest of my life, banging my head against the carpet trying to find the right chord," he recalls in an interview in *Details* ("Sincerely, L. Cohen" 102). More pointedly, he explains elsewhere that "I was trying to come up with a solution to being a writer and not having to go to a university to teach" (qtd. in Browne 28). Early critics of his music, however, could not understand his modulated sounds and subdominant or dominant keys, nor could they respond to what he describes as his effort to write verses with "the same lyric limpidness as some of the Scottish Border ballads or Irish songs, and later some of the Spanish Civil War songs" ("Sincerely, L. Cohen" 102).

The development of Cohen's singing career along with what has been labelled "folk-poetry" in the late sixties seemed to fulfil his need to link the spiritual with the hip. But Cohen became the subject of much criticism for this union, which "Beautiful Creep," the title of an article by Richard Goldstein in the *Village Voice*, documents. Published in December 1967, it castigates Cohen for being "a Visceral Romantic" who "suffers gloriously in every couplet" (41). Goldstein doubts that "he has always written with a typewriter for a guitar" and offers a description of Cohen slaving away, one word at a time, over a set of new songs, "trying to make them sound the way they read" (41, 44). These criticisms led partly to the clichés about his songwriting and singing, *The Penguin Encyclopedia of Popular Music*, for example, labelling him "bard of bedsits" and journalists gleefully describing his songs as "music to slit your wrists by." Some quipped that Cohen's music could only be listened to in cloudy

weather. Neglecting such criticism, Cohen celebrated his
to pop culture because, he says, "It's an assault on history and
it's an assault on all these authoritarian voices who have always
told us what was beautiful" ("After the Wipe-Out").

What Goldstein's article did expose was Cohen's abiding dedication to songwriting, which takes time and more time. He
explains in 1993 that "Composing hardly begins to describe what
the process is. It's something like scavenging, something like
farming in sand, something like scraping the bottom of the
barrel. The process doesn't have any dignity. It is work of
extreme poverty" (qtd. in Pearson 76). Part of the intensity of
the struggle is that his standards are severe, but Cohen knows
that a song will yield itself if he sticks with it long enough.
"Anthem," from *The Future*, began in the early 1980s, and he first
thought it would fit on *Various Positions* (1985) and then, possibly,
on *I'm Your Man* (1988). It wasn't ready until 1992. "Democracy,"
also from *The Future*, similarly took time, three years to be exact.

Despite the intensity of his process of musical composition,
Cohen persistently believes there is no difference between a
poem and a song. "All of my writing has guitars behind it, even
the novels," he declared in 1969 (qtd. in Murphy 48). But part of
the mystery of Cohen's songwriting is his belief that from a
certain point of view his songs have no meaning: "There's not a
secret that is being concealed, there's nothing that I am not
yielding. . . . Sometimes I feel like my work is like an ice cube . . .
you can put it in a Coke or you can put it in a scotch . . . it just
has an effect, it's hard to say what it's getting at, I'm not sure it's
getting *at* anything *but* an effect . . ." ("Sincerely, L. Cohen" 104).

A few key appearances in 1967 created such an effect. The
crucial appearance, perhaps, occurred on 30 April 1967 at New
York's Town Hall at a concert for SANE against the Vietnam War
and was broadcast on radio. In her autobiography, *Trust Your
Heart*, Collins recounts Cohen's anxiety about performing. He
nervously walked onto the stage in an elegant suit and, with
hands and legs shaking, began "Suzanne," but he stopped half-
way into the first verse, whispered into the microphone that he

FIGURE 8

*Cohen, in a publicity shot in 1967, at
the beginning of his musical career.*

couldn't go on, and left the stage. The audience called him back, but his stage fright prevailed. Only at the urging of Collins and in response to the shouting audience did he return: "He shook himself and drew his body up and put his shoulders back, smiled again, and walked back onto the stage. He finished 'Suzanne,' and the audience went wild. He has been giving concerts ever since" (146). Other accounts, however, suggest that this incident occurred at the Rheingold Music Festival that summer in Central Park.

Cohen's public appearances that summer were few — his next performance was at the Newport Folk Festival on 16 July. A backstage photograph from Newport captures a youthful singer nervously waiting for his cue with a heavy guitar slung upside down over his shoulder, standing behind and off to the side of the other entertainers, who included Joan Baez. Cohen was lionized at the Newport concert, even though, while travelling there with his lawyer Marty Machat, he had confided to him that he didn't really know how to sing. "None of you guys know how to sing," his lawyer had responded, adding, Cohen recalls, "When I want to hear singers, I go to the Metropolitan Opera" (qtd. in Ruhlmann 11). But Cohen's sensibility, with its roots in literature, poetry, and religion, influenced by the Beats, Dylan, and the world of Montreal, and buttressed by his absorption with the erotic and the violent, found a devoted, nearly cult following that continues today.

By late 1967 Cohen completed the recording of his first album at Columbia Records's Studio E in New York. Prosaically entitled *Songs of Leonard Cohen*, the album, like his poetry, elaborates personal themes, which at that time included his relationships with women, particularly with Marianne. Of the ten songs on the album, four refer directly to women in their titles, including "Suzanne," "Sisters of Mercy," and "So Long, Marianne." Four others have women as central figures. The songs' origins vary from an encounter with a Montreal dancer to the two young, homeless women (Barbara and Lorraine) whom Cohen met in Edmonton one winter night and invited to sleep in his hotel room, watching over them — the source for "Sisters of Mercy," which he wrote in one night, an unusual experience for him, he explained to the critic Alan Twigg ("Leonard Cohen" 44–45).

Criticized for being a mediocre musician because he limits himself to only three or four chords, Cohen whimsically defends himself by saying, "I have merely decided to opt for the greatest simplicity" ("Leonard Cohen" 46). At the time of his first album, Cohen also lost the rights to "Suzanne" and has never benefited from its being frequently recorded by others; he responded, however, by forming his own company, called Stranger Music, which copyrights all his songs. The name derives from "The Stranger Song," the first composition that he performed in concert and that he recorded on his first album; ironically, though, he also lost copyright for this song. Unofficially released on 26 December 1967, *Songs of Leonard Cohen* appeared within a month of Dylan's *John Wesley Harding* — and became a modest success (Ruhlmann 15).

The album notes fail to record that by 1967 Cohen and Marianne were drifting apart, although "So Long, Marianne" provides more than a hint. Living near Clinton Street on the lower east side of New York, Cohen was separated from Montreal, Hydra, and Marianne. A sense of loss and loneliness followed their parting, which occurred throughout 1966 and 1967, with Marianne finally returning to Oslo after Cohen moved to Franklin, Tennessee, in 1968 to record his second album, *Songs from a Room* (1969). He had begun "So Long, Marianne" in Montreal and completed it at the Chelsea, and, although they were still occasionally seeing each other in New York, Cohen understood that he and Marianne could not continue in such an unstable state because it interfered with his clarity of purpose. As he writes in the song,

You know I love to live with you,
But you make me forget so very much
I forget to pray for the angel
and then the angels forget to pray for us.

FIGURE 9

Cohen in Franklin, Tennessee, in 1968 during the recording of Songs from a Room.

The seventh verse, printed in *Stranger Music* but not recorded, despairingly asks, "How come you gave your news to everyone / when you said it was a secret just for me[?]" (101). The chorus originally read, "My father is falling / but my grandfather is calling," a testimony to Cohen's attachment to the memory of his maternal grandfather, Rabbi Solomon Klinitsky-Klein. "Hey, That's No Way to Say Goodbye," written at the Penn Terminal Hotel on 34th Street in 1966, elaborates the sense of loss and separation that was descending on Cohen and Marianne; indeed, a powerful loneliness pervades the album.

During this period of separation and withdrawal, drugs played an increasingly larger part in Cohen's life. On Hydra they were recreational and largely hashish, but in New York he depended on them. Speed and LSD were part of the scene at the Chelsea. To escape them, Cohen moved for awhile to the Henry Hudson Hotel on West 58th Street, but he could not so easily shake his habit.

Cohen's wish to reach a wider audience was beginning to be realized, notably through the various cover songs by musicians such as Judy Collins, Joe Cocker, Diana Ross, and Neil Diamond, who all did versions of "Bird on the Wire," and Buffy Sainte-Marie, who recorded the "God is alive. Magic is afoot" section from *Beautiful Losers* for Vanguard. Richie Havens, Joni Mitchell, Jennifer Warnes, Rita Coolidge, Suzanne Vega, Tracy Chapman, and Nick Cave have all done cover versions of Cohen songs, and the trend continues beyond the success of the 1991 *I'm Your Fan* tribute album with Emmy Lou Harris's version of "Ballad of a Run Away Pony" in 1993.

The change from poetry to songwriting was a move that saved Cohen's creative life. Although the period from 1967 to 1993 saw only a limited number of his books published, it marks not only his productive recording years, culminating in such outstanding albums as *I'm Your Man* (1988) and *The Future* (1992), but also the emergence and solidification of his worldwide reputation. Music has been the vehicle that has made it possible for Cohen not only to grow but also to stay before the public, reaching larger and more diverse audiences than one composed of readers alone. He summarized the importance of this situation before a national audience at the 1991 Juno Awards: "To place a song into the air and have it last twenty years — that's a wonderful thing."

Cohen's popularity as a singer, however, jeopardized if not undermined his reputation as a writer. Yet the spare melodies and rich imagery of his songs extend the lyricism of his early poetry, and the seriousness of his narrative songs and ballads reflects the constant spirituality and angst of his writing, represented by the trilogy of texts published since *Selected Poems: 1956–1968*: *The Energy of Slaves* (1972), *Death of a Lady's Man* (1978), and *Book of Mercy* (1984). Read in conjunction with his development as a songwriter, these books confirm the strong connection between his singing and writing. But in drawing on a Quebec folk tradition of ballads, mixed with the French technique and tone of the *chanson* and leavened with a touch of politics and pop, Cohen has established an unmusical but unique sound that has been surprisingly successful.

In August 1968, a summary article in the *New York Times* identified the work of Bob Dylan, Paul Simon, Laura Nyro, Rod McKuen, and Leonard Cohen as representative of the best in a new merging of poetry and popular music. *Maclean's* similarly celebrated Cohen's new status, regarding him as Canada's answer to Dylan. Capitalizing on this popularity was the publication of *Selected Poems 1956–1968* (1968). A collection of material from Cohen's first four books, plus twenty new poems, the work was an immediate bestseller in Canada and the United States, appearing in England the following year and then in translation: in German (1971), Hebrew (1971), Swedish (1972), French (1972), and Spanish (1974). Reviews appeared in *Time*, the *Washington Post*, *Le devoir*, and the publishing industry's book service, the *Kirkus Reviews*, although it mistakenly reviewed the book in the juvenile section. Marianne selected the poems in the collection, perhaps the greatest compliment Cohen ever paid to her.

Selected Poems 1956–1968 is a survey of Cohen's most valuable work, beginning with "For Wilf and His House," the second poem in his first book, *Let Us Compare Mythologies*, and ending with "He Studies to Describe." The two poems are instructive, for in the first Cohen draws on Christian imagery, biblical narrative, personal suffering, and the nature of modern loneliness: "Now each in his holy hill / the glittering and hurting days are almost done. / Then let us compare mythologies" (*Selected Poems* 3). "He Studies to Describe" shifts from first- to third-person narrative and outlines the efforts of the subject to become "the lover he cannot become / failing the widest dreams of the mind / & settling for visions of God" (239). Trust and love are paramount, expressed in a tone of quiet despair. Mythology has been replaced by intense self-scrutiny.

The volume presents an arc that originates in loss, has a momentary triumph in love, but ends in pain; or, as "This Is for You" expresses, "All this happened / in the truth of time / in the truth of flesh" (221). Contradictions, however, have overtaken the narrator's life: "Now I am a shadow / I long for the boundaries / of my wandering" (222). The lyricism balancing the anguish enhanced the appeal of the collection, solidifying Cohen's reputation as a writer of suffering and feeling. "New Poems," at the end of the book, provided a sense of fresh directions in form, although not in theme. The penultimate poem, "Marita," for example, is a characteristically comic plea — "MARITA / PLEASE FIND ME / I AM ALMOST 30" (239) — and was first written with a felt pen on the cement wall of a Montreal sidewalk café and filmed in *Ladies and Gentlemen . . . Mr. Leonard Cohen* (Owen 32). Such humour balances the final and moving poem, "He Studies to Describe."

The success of *Selected Poems 1956–1968* was immediate — it sold nearly 200,000 copies in the first three months after its publication. Critics responded to the personal voice, Kenneth Rexroth claiming that Cohen's new "people poetry — direct, one to the other, I to Thou," was a "breakthrough" (qtd. in Dorman 213). Chad Walsh, quoted in a Viking Press ad for *Selected Poems 1956–1968*, declares that "His [Cohen's] love poems have the sensuous lyricism of Theodore Roethke with a dash of the Song

An Original Publication/$2.50

LEONARD COHEN
SELECTED POEMS
1956-1968

FIGURE IO

The cover of Selected Poems 1956–1968: *the book won the Governor General's Literary Award for English-language poetry, but Cohen declined the award.*

of Solomon." This ad, in the *New York Times*, includes "A modern housewife's lament, plucked from *New York* magazine": "It's so difficult, you know, wearing mini-skirts and keeping up with Leonard Cohen, and not going insane when the diaper service doesn't come" (advertisement). One recalls the appropriateness of Cohen's remark, "I've always depended on the kindness of women" (qtd. in Dorman 189).

In April 1969, the Canada Council announced its Governor General's Literary Awards, and Cohen was among the winners. He found the acclaim flattering but could not accept the award, declaring in a well-publicized remark via telegram, "Though much in me craves this award, the poems themselves absolutely forbid it" (qtd. in Teitelbaum). But he was not alone in declining the award that year. Hubert Aquin also refused to accept the prize because he was a separatist and a member of the Rassemblement pour l'indépendance nationale. The embarrassment caused by two winners refusing the award led to a new policy of privately consulting with winners about whether they intended to accept the award. Chair of the English-language jury the year that Cohen declined the prize was Robert Weaver of the CBC; Henry Kreisel and Philip Stratford completed the membership.

The evening of the awards ceremony, the brash thirty-three-year-old poet attended a party given by Jack McClelland at an Ottawa hotel, where Mordecai Richler, upon seeing him, motioned him into a bathroom and sternly asked him why he had refused the award. "I don't know," Cohen replied; "Any other answer and I would have punched you in the nose," the startled Richler shot back (qtd. in Teitelbaum 22).

The publication of *Selected Poems 1956–1968* marked a hiatus in Cohen's writing as he "disappeared onto the public stage" (Hutcheon, "Leonard Cohen (1934–)" [Fiction Series] 26), which limited his literary productivity: *The Energy of Slaves* did not appear until 1972; six years later saw *Death of a Lady's Man*; and six years after that, *Book of Mercy* appeared. A new collection, *Stranger Music: Selected Poems and Songs*, appeared in November 1993, nine years after Cohen's last title. Such interruption and silence, however, are characteristic of Cohen's determined but intermittent productivity.

Two British Broadcasting Corporation shows in 1968 became a forum for some of the soon-to-be released songs on Cohen's second album, *Songs from a Room* (1969), which climbed to number sixty-three on the *Billboard* top two hundred soon after its appearance and to number two on the charts in England. While lacking the variety of the first album, it possessed a set of risky lyrics, including "Seems So Long Ago, Nancy," in which Cohen sings about her suicide; "The Butcher," in which he sings,

I found a needle
I put into my arm
It did some good
Did some harm;

and "You Know Who I Am," in which he sings about child-killing. The quintessential Cohen song — thoughtful, engaged, frightening, and musically austere — emerged: "Bird on the Wire," "Story of Isaac," "The Partisan," and "The Old Revolution" all made their debut on this second album. In addition to its commercial and critical success, it achieved Cohen's goal of being recorded in Nashville with his own group, called simply The Army. Yet a tone of loss pervades the general lack of tempo and focus on either personal separation or political defeat, embodied in a single, desolate space, a room: laconically, Cohen laments in "Tonight Will Be Fine" that "There's only one prayer / And I listen all night / For your step on the stair." But in "The Old Revolution" he exclaims that "even damnation is poisoned with rainbows." The album concludes with a remarkable disappearance: after the last verse of "Tonight Will Be Fine," the song ends with Cohen humming, then whistling, and then silent. It is as if words can no longer be found to convey his despair.

During this period, and coinciding with his move to Tennessee, Cohen began a new relationship with Suzanne Elrod, a brunette who became the mother of his two children: Adam Nathan (born in 1972) and Lorca Sarah (born in 1974). Cohen and

Suzanne met in New York at a Scientology meeting, and her picture appears on the 1977 album *Death of a Ladies' Man* alongside of Cohen and Eva La Pierre. In Tennessee, he rented a farm from the songwriter Boudleaux Bryant, who wrote "Bye Bye Love" for the Everly Brothers. Cohen's producer at the time, Bob Johnston, introduced him to Bryant, from whom Cohen rented what he called a hut for seventy-five dollars a month: "I had a house, a jeep, a rifle, a pair of cowboy boots, a girlfriend. . . . A typewriter, a guitar. Everything I needed," he told a French interviewer some years later ("Comme un guerrier" 62). But inland at Franklin, Tennessee, he missed the cosmopolitanism of New York and the island world of Hydra. Only a featureless plain surrounded him on the 1,500 acres. Horseback riding and shooting became his avocations — in France he would actually appear at a concert on a white horse.

Cohen continued his spiritual self-examination at this period of despair and disappointment; rumours of an attempted suicide began to circulate. The opening lines of "For a long time / he had no music / he had no scenery," in *The Energy of Slaves* (120), express this paralysis, tempered only when he encountered Rinzai Buddhism through the master or Roshi, Joshu Sasaki. A Japanese Zen Buddhist who had left his monastery to come to America in 1962, Roshi met Cohen through Steve Sanfield, who knew of Roshi's monastery at Mt. Baldy, northeast of Los Angeles. Cohen visited it for a four-week trial. His initial reaction was tempered: he valued the liberation of the mind but found the discipline of the body too challenging. A second trip to Mt. Baldy affirmed the importance of Buddhist exercises and spirituality for Cohen, and it initiated a constant reorientation and recovery of self-discipline at the monastery from 1970 to the present. Cohen has sometimes remained there for up to three months. Self-examination is the key to this training in how to deal with the outside world, with self-satisfaction and complacency. Annihilating what interferes with the essential self is the goal, something that Cohen has emphasized in the process of songwriting and the intensity required to get to the words.

Renamed in the tradition of Rinzai Buddhism, Cohen was called "Solitary Cliff." Although he was later sceptical about some aspects of Buddhism, his involvement with the discipline of Rinzai Buddhism continues, as does his commitment to Roshi.

In 1969 Cohen decided to establish a firmer base in Montreal, taking a small house in the "Greek" district of the city, the Mount Royal and Park Avenue section, anticipating a more permanent return. He was criticized, however, for staying in Greece after the April 1969 coup despite his own danger and his knowledge of how some of his friends had been tortured. Two poems beginning "I threw open the shutters" in *The Energy of Slaves* record these events (10–11). Cohen justified his irregular visits to Hydra after the coup by explaining that it was not "a betrayal of mankind to vacation in a country ruled by fascists" because "I didn't see it that way. I had a house there, friends; I didn't consider presence there a collaboration. It was the contrary" ("Comme un guerrier" 62).

Confirming Cohen's musical growth was the appearance in 1969 of the book *Songs of Leonard Cohen*, which contains arrangements from his first two albums and uses the photo from *Songs from a Room* — Cohen in his cowboy hat — for the title page. Beginning with a reprint of William Kloman's 1968 *New York Times* article, the book then presents a series of photographs of Cohen in Greece, Montreal, Nashville, and New York often with Marianne Jensen, John Hammond, and Judy Collins. The music for twenty songs follows, beginning with "Bird on the Wire" and including "A Bunch of Lonesome Heroes," "Suzanne," "You Know Who I Am," "Sisters of Mercy," "So Long, Marianne," "The Stranger Song," and "The Butcher," with its concluding lines,

I'm broken down
From a recent fall.
Blood upon my body
And ice upon my soul
Lead on, my son, it is your world. (96)

The book made accessible the range of Cohen's music and verse while clarifying biographical details such as his vegetarianism between 1965 and 1968.

NEW AUDIENCES

Cohen's first European tour, in May 1970, followed, consisting of seven shows, beginning in Hamburg. The day after a concert at the Royal Albert Hall, London (10 May), he gave a poetry reading at the Institute of Contemporary Arts. Evoking his Judaic past was the opening song for each concert, "Un as der rebbe singt" ("As the Rabbi Sings"). "Bird on the Wire," "So Long, Marianne," and "You Know Who I Am" followed — until twenty songs were presented, with "Suzanne" the nineteenth and "Please Don't Pass Me By" the twentieth.

The tour was a success: at the concluding concert, held at the Olympia in Paris on 13 May 1970, police had to be called in to calm the crowd after many fans had joined Cohen on stage at his request. And it was soon said "that if any young French woman owned but one record," it was likely to be by Leonard Cohen (Fetherling 33), who was named "le folksinger de l'année" by Le nouvel observateur that year. In France he was later a guest of both President Giscard d'Estaing and his successor, Georges Pompidou, who, reportedly, often took Cohen's records with him on vacations. The enthusiasm generated by this early tour did not diminish, and Cohen's later European concerts were constantly greeted by excited crowds that, as in the Royal Albert Hall, London, in May 1993, gave him a standing ovation before he sang a single word or played a single note.

Returning to the United States, Cohen performed at a folk festival held at the Forest Hills Tennis stadium in New York on 25 July. By 2 August, however, he was back in Europe, singing at a festival in Aix-en-Provence, where he arrived on the stage riding a white horse. The crowd, but not his musicians, found this manner of entry unusual: the players were all from Texas and Tennessee and regularly rode horses; the French found it charmingly unorthodox. But when the crowd began to yell "Fascist!" at Cohen for his failure to protest the 1969 generals' coup in Greece, which defeated the Papandreou government, the concert faltered. Cohen, however, stood up to the shouting, telling the fans to take the microphone if they were displeased with his performance. They did not, and he performed eleven songs, six of them solo, comically titling a short improvisation "I Don't Know What I Wanna Sing." The concert, heard on French AM radio, further magnified his European reputation.

On 31 August Cohen performed at the Isle of Wight, sharing the program with The Doors, Miles Davis, and Jimi Hendrix. He recited three poems and performed fourteen songs at the open-air concert. The poems were "Dead Song," "They Locked Up a Man," and "A Person Who Eats Meat." Afterward, Cohen read what he still believes to be the worst review he has ever received: "Leonard Cohen," wrote a British journalist in *Melody Maker*, "is an old bore who should just return to Canada which he never should have left to begin with" ("Comme un guerrier" 62). However, a measure of his increasing popularity in Canada was the production of *The Shining People of Leonard Cohen*, the Royal Winnipeg Ballet's interpretation of his early love lyrics; it premièred in Paris in June before a thunderous audience and was later presented at the National Arts Centre in Ottawa.

Earlier, in March 1970, Cohen had begun recording his third album, *Songs of Love and Hate*, in Nashville, enlarging his sound with the accompaniment of strings and the backup voices of two female vocalists. A children's choir had also been dubbed in on "Last Year's Man" and "Dress Rehearsal Rag." Released in 1971, the album contains two of Cohen's signature songs: "Famous Blue Raincoat" and "Joan of Arc," the latter inspired by Nico, Andy Warhol's companion. For that song Cohen had employed an unusual recording approach, using overlapping tracks of him singing and speaking the lyrics. It was enormously effective. A number of the songs had again taken months, even years, to

FIGURE II

Cohen performing at the Isle of Wight in 1970.

complete: Cohen first performed "Dress Rehearsal Rag" in 1968; "Last Year's Man" took him five years to write.

The songs attempt to overcome the weaknesses of his first two albums, essentially the overextension of metaphor and the sudden shifting from one conceit to another, compensated by too much repetition in the melody line. In *Songs of Love and Hate*, however, longer, slower songs dominate; they are more ponderous in tone, with less romantic patterns of imagery. "Avalanche" and "Dress Rehearsal Rag" illustrate this change well. Additionally, Cohen's conscious effort to be identified as an intellectual and a composer of serious songs is very evident. Taking the romantic viewpoint of French singers, such as Jacques Brel, and covering it with a "poetic religiosity" that expresses "sorrow at the human condition," Cohen created a sound that embodies a distinctive, and oddly attractive, sombre temperament (Fetherling 45).

While working on the album in the spring of 1970, Cohen was honoured by the academic establishment: he received an honorary doctorate from Dalhousie University in Halifax that May. The citation states that, for many, "Leonard Cohen has become a symbol of their own anguish, alienation and uncertainty." *Beautiful Losers* "established him as the mouthpiece of the confusion and uncertainty felt by a whole generation," and his "albums are outstandingly popular with the young of the seventies" (qtd. in Dorman 233–34). Rarely had one who supposedly stood at the margin of society been recognized by one of its institutions.

Throughout that year Cohen performed and continued to perfect his sound. He returned to Montreal on 10 December to give a concert, at the Place des Arts, billed as "Leonard Cohen and The Nashville Army." The public and the press celebrated him, as they had at Massey Hall in Toronto and at Carleton University in Ottawa, before his Montreal performance. Underscoring his stature was his choice as "Entertainer of the Year" by the *Globe and Mail* on 25 December 1970 (Batten). The basis of its decision was his presence and intelligence, which more than made up for his voice, it explained. Cohen himself later quipped that, although his voice is not the finest, he does have a certain way of delivering a song.

The 1971 release of *Songs of Love and Hate*, however, demonstrated how easily one's popularity can be undone. The album, one of almost pure dejection, with Cohen expressing dissatisfaction with himself and with life, initiated nearly a decade of despair. In his words, his voice is "wiped out," full of conflict and anxiety, and the album is inauthentic (qtd. in Dorman 234, 235). Angst, not sadness, emanates from the songs, which convey his unhappiness and internal conflict even while he was being acknowledged as a pop icon. Critics warned that it was impossible to listen to a Cohen album while the sun was shining. The songs no longer resolved the pain that he felt; and while *Songs of Leonard Cohen* and *Songs from a Room* had gone gold in Canada, for sales over 100,000, *Songs of Love and Hate* did not, even given a commercial push from Columbia. Publication of the arrangements for voice and guitar, also entitled *Songs of Love and Hate* (1972), with a reprint of "Ladies and Gents, Leonard Cohen," by Jack Hafferkamp of *Rolling Stone*, did little to improve sales.

Projecting an intimacy often allegorically expressed, Cohen was an individual who felt compromised by his inability to experience the intensity of life. The opening lines of "Avalanche," published as a poem in *Parasites of Heaven*, are representative: "I stepped into an avalanche / It covered up my soul"; Cohen closes the first verse with, "You who wish to conquer pain / Must learn to serve me well" (78). "Famous Blue Raincoat," based on a Burberry that he had purchased in London in 1959, is a well-recorded lament. Cohen says in the liner notes of *The Best of Leonard Cohen* that Elizabeth, his friend at the time, "thought I looked like a spider in it. That was probably why she wouldn't go to Greece with me. It hung more heroically when I took out the lining, and achieved glory when the frayed sleeves were repaired with a little leather." It was stolen from Marianne's loft in New York in the early seventies.

Coinciding with the release of the album was Cohen's music

FIGURE 12

*Cohen performing at the Salle Wilfrid
Pelletier on 10 December 1970.*

on the soundtrack of Robert Altman's film *McCabe and Mrs. Miller*, starring Warren Beatty and Julie Christie. Altman used "The Stranger Song," "Sisters of Mercy," and "Winter Lady," all from *Songs of Leonard Cohen*, and two instrumental tracks were especially recorded for the soundtrack in a New York studio. Cohen's craggy voice, which Jay Cocks describes as sounding "like Villon with frostbite," was appropriate for this western romance, shot in the mountains above Vancouver. The movie, however, flopped and has still failed to earn a million dollars in gross receipts, according to Altman, who recently called it "the biggest failure of all my films." Yet, in this 1993 interview, he ironically noted that "it is on the list of the best 25 pictures of the last 25 years."

In the winter of 1972, Cohen decided to settle in Montreal, purchasing a two-storey house on rue Vallières, between Boulevard St-Laurent and rue St-Dominique, facing Parc Portugal. He felt that it was time to stop roaming, staying no longer than a month in one place over the preceding four years. But why Montreal? According to Cohen, "When a guy gets attached to a city, it becomes a city of the mind. I still have this notion of Montreal as the capital of the sentimental world — the atmosphere here is romantic. . . . I was formed by this place . . ." (qtd. in Kapica). He also felt that being in the city would reduce his natural laziness.

At this time, preceding his second European tour, in March and April 1972, which also took Cohen to Israel, he practised yoga, gave up drugs, fasted, and exercised. His relationship with Suzanne was strong and, despite his ongoing inner searching, he seemed satisfied with his career. At thirty-seven, Cohen was fit, relatively happy, and productive. Time spent in and out of the Buddhist monastery on Mt. Baldy was satisfying, and a new Toyota jeep made the travelling easier. Following an assessment of his papers (purchased by the University of Toronto), he headed to the monastery in California for five weeks and then, in March, to Nashville to rehearse with a new band before starting the tour of twenty-three European cities in forty days.

In Studio A of Columbia Records in Nashville, Cohen worked hard to find the right mix, unhappily dismissing the two original female vocalists who were to join him on the tour because their voices did not mesh with his. Two new singers (one of them, Jennifer Warren, later known as Jennifer Warnes) joined him a few days later, and they clicked. From his first to his most recent tour, Cohen has used two female backup singers because, he once ironically remarked, his voice "depresses" him, and he needs their coloratura (qtd. in Saltzman 80). With daily workouts at the YMCA, he was able to adjust his physical needs with his mental demands. Yet, in the early seventies, he felt uncomfortable with his new luxury, explaining to Paul Saltzman that

My standard of living went down as my income increased. . . . I lived a lot better when I had no money. I was living in a beautiful big house on a Greek Island. I was swimming every day; writing, working, meeting people from over the whole world and moving around with tremendous mobility. . . . Now . . . I find myself living in hotel rooms, breathing bad air, and very constrained as to movement. (78)

Cohen added that he had just finished writing *The Energy of Slaves*, a collection of eighty poems, "to represent the situation of where I am right now. That to me totally acquits me of any responsibility I have of keeping a record public" (79).

In Hydra, just before commencing the tour, Cohen spent time regaining his emotional direction in preparation for the strain of touring, which at this time he did not enjoy. Stopping in London on his return to the United States, he planned a film of his tour, to be produced by his new company, appropriately called Sincere Productions. In an interview with a British journalist, Cohen reiterated his belief that people were living in a period of judgement and thus sensing that they were getting to the end of things: "this is not the time to put anybody on," he declared (qtd. in Dorman 241). Twenty years later, he still echoed this sentiment. His self-deprecating comment on *Songs of Love and Hate*, released in January-February 1971, indicates his unease with the project: "the same old droning work, an inch or two forward." He also noted at that time that he was considering withdrawing from his publishers a manuscript called "Songs of Disobedience," which he in fact did; it later appeared, however, as *The Energy of Slaves*, published in 1972.

With a close-cropped Buddhist haircut, Cohen undertook his second European tour, beginning in Dublin and stopping, among other cities, in London, Copenhagen, Stockholm, Frankfurt, Berlin, Vienna, Geneva, and Paris. The tour continued to Jerusalem and Tel Aviv. In Israel in April 1972, he broke all attendance records; in Tel Aviv, between two and three thousand fans were expected to turn up; ten thousand appeared, and, to ease the pressure, Cohen invited them to move closer to the stage. Chaos ensued, although order was eventually restored. To maintain the intensity of his Israeli performances, he dropped some acid (he had earlier used dangerous amounts of speed to complete *Beautiful Losers*). In Jerusalem, he appeared on stage apparently drugged and was in tears by the time he came to sing "So Long, Marianne." But with Jennifer Warnes and Donna Washburn as backup singers, and regulars such as Ron Cornelius and Bob Johnston, producer as well as keyboard player, The Army solidified Cohen's concert successes, in no small part due to an expanded repertoire, which averaged seventeen songs a performance and numerous encores, a Cohen trademark.

The end of the tour, however, brought self-doubt and the need to reassess. Cohen returned to Hydra — having given up his lease at the Franklin, Tennessee, farm, but still owning a house in Montreal — and stated that he was abandoning popular music. The birth of his children during this period disrupted his focus on art, and, as he saw his freedom slipping away and his identity changing, he realized that his relationship with Suzanne was altering. His work at this time, "A Woman Being Born," then changed to "My Life in Art" — both source texts for *Death of a Lady's Man* (1978) — reflects this change. These titles sharply summarize his dual stance as a self-conscious romantic and a postmodern creator: the poet as both public artist and private lover.

The Energy of Slaves appeared at this time with a remarkable photo on the back cover of an aggressive, glaring Cohen. The text confirms the sense of anger and desolation that he was personally experiencing despite his public success. On *Adrienne Clarkson Presents: Leonard Cohen*, he called *The Energy of Slaves* "a raw" book, one that openly records his pain. He was anxious about its reception, believing in March 1972 that publishing it might have been "a mistake" (qtd. in Saltzman 80). In the photograph, Cohen stands with a shaved head, like a convict or a penitent, in a bathroom, but he could as easily be standing in a morgue. Yet he is unrelenting in his aggressiveness, linking the tone of the poems to the image of the poet and the failure of aesthetic expression and human emotion.

The narcissism and rhetoric of failure disappointed reviewers, who tended to take the statements of failure in the poems at face value, unable to recognize, as critic Eli Mandel remarks, that Cohen was demonstrating that "art has the capacity to contain its own contradiction" (135). The antipoems of the text moved Cohen far from the lyricism of his first two books and the historicism of his next two, *Flowers for Hitler* and *Parasites of Heaven*. In contrast, a powerful subjectivism and anger erupt, entrapping the narrator and departing from the seemingly conventional verse and tone in *Selected Poems 1956–1968*. Even the humour in the collection is mordant, as in the wonderfully entitled "On Hearing that Irving Layton Was Kissed by Allen Ginsberg at a Toronto Poetry Reading" (98), actually a warning for Layton. There is little of the inauthentic in this writing, although one must always guard against the con, as Cohen reminded a *Maclean's* journalist in June 1972, adding that "There's no story so fantastic that I cannot imagine myself the hero. And there's no story so evil that I cannot imagine myself the villain" (qtd. in Saltzman 6).

The Energy of Slaves registers a dual loss: of art and of love, which often disappear together, as in "The Progress of My Style" (52). Such loss can only be recovered by the facing poems, which frequently accompany and/or revise the original work and possibly bridge or destroy the gap between art and desire. Living with a woman in Montreal, Cohen has lost his inspiration, finding "no altar for my song" (52). But following this titled poem — there are only twelve with titles in the collection — is an untitled one with a razor blade as a symbol and these startling, angry lines:

> I dream of torturing you
> because you are so puffed up with pride
> You stand there with a bill of rights
> or an automatic rifle.

The narrator then becomes a Miltonic "angel of revenge" (53), striking out against the emotional and artistic injustice he feels. The struggle is that Cohen is wanted, but ". . . without my agony / without the risk," and "without my prophet's mantle / without my loneliness," as he later writes. This "loneliness" cannot be sacrificed, however, because it would mean abandoning his art (90). Such dismemberment disgraces poetry, which can no longer be written because "The poems don't love us anymore" (117). Empty and exhausted, the poet even considers renouncing his name:

> I have no talent left
> I can't write a poem anymore
> You can call me Len or Lennie now
> like you always wanted
> I guess I should pack it up
> but habits persist. (112)

Punishment by art is the price he pays as he becomes a slave seeking invention (95). In crossing Arthur Rimbaud with Louis-Ferdinand Céline, Cohen daringly undermines the very discipline — poetry — that has established his identity. The angry and savage deconstruction of his aesthetic, however, was a necessary stage, continued in his next book, *Death of a Lady's Man*, which appeared six years later. Both works were preparatory to his claim of resurrection through prayer in *Book of Mercy* (1984). After the mythology and lyricism of Cohen's first two books had been made transparent by the historical realities in *Flowers for Hitler* and *Parasites of Heaven*, Cohen plunged thematically into the inferno of self and self-hatred in *The Energy of Slaves*. He then rose toward purgatory in *Death of a Lady's Man* before approaching paradise in *Book of Mercy*. Despair in *The Energy of Slaves* translates into opportunity in *Death of a Lady's Man* (see *"Your Moment Now"* [14]), reflecting the irony and inversion present throughout Cohen's writing — in practical terms, *Energy*/energy creates only spiritual and poetic anger or paralysis while *Death*/death provides a glimpse of life.

Both endurance and vulnerability characterize Cohen, although at times he has doubted their power, as when his support for the British Black Muslim leader, Michael Malik (Michael X), through letters and public statements, did not help to stop Malik's execution in Trinidad after being arrested on trumped-up charges (Collins 147–48). Disillusionment began to overcome Cohen's work and, preceding the release of *Live Songs* in April 1973, his fourth album, rumours of his retirement from music began to circulate. They originated in the misrepresentation of his remarks to a rock journalist for the British pop paper, *Melody Maker*. By January his agent had to assure many fans that Cohen was not leaving the scene for a Buddhist monastery. Cohen had meant to convey that he was "experiencing a boredom over the state of music. . . . There was an energy in songs in 1966, but it seems to have gone, all the emotions are lost. That's all I said," he told a Montreal reporter in 1973 (qtd. in Kapica).

Live Songs contradicted the rumours of Cohen's retirement. A compilation of songs performed largely during his 1970 and 1972 tours, the album met with unwelcome press but popular acceptance. Its tone was still sombre, and the cover said it all: Cohen

LEONARD COHEN: LIVE SONGS

SIDE ONE:

1. Minute Prologue
London 1972
2. Passing Thru
London 1972
3. You Know Who I Am
Brussels 1972
4. Bird on the Wire
Paris 1972
5. Nancy
London 1972
6. Improvisation
Paris 1972

SIDE TWO:

1. Story of Isaac
Berlin 1972
2. Please Don't Pass Me By
(A Disgrace)
London 1970
3. Tonight Will Be Fine
Isle of Wight 1970
4. Queen Victoria
Room in Tennessee 1972

Produced by Bob Johnston
Bob Potter: Engineer
All songs
Stranger Music Inc.(BMI)
Cover photograph by S. B. Elrod

MUSICIANS 1972
Ron Cornelius
Acoustic and Electric Guitar
Peter Marshal
Stand-up and Electric Bass
David O'Connor
Acoustic Guitar
Bob Johnston
Organ
Leonard Cohen
Acoustic Guitar
Donna Washburn
Vocals
Jennifer Warren
Vocals

MUSICIANS 1970
Ron Cornelius
Electric Guitar
Charlie Daniels
Electric Bass
and Fiddle
Elkin Fowler
Banjo and Guitar
Bob Johnston
Harmonica and Guitar
Leonard Cohen
Acoustic Guitar
Aileen Fowler
Vocals
Corlynn Hanney
Vocals

FIGURE 13

The cover of Cohen's 1973 album, Live Songs: *the picture first appeared as the jacket photo of* The Energy of Slaves *(1972).*

with a Buddhist haircut aggressively staring at the camera while standing in a nondescript, tiled room. The look is tough, abrasive, and threatening, the songs likewise. The picture made a statement, one that Cohen favoured at the time, having also used the image on the jacket of *The Energy of Slaves*. The publication on the back of the album of two poems, "Transfiguration" and "Intensity," by the minor British artist Daphne Richardson, who had died in 1972, testifies to Cohen's sensitivity to suffering.

The opening song, "Minute Prologue," suggests that Cohen's music can heal the dissension, pain, and hurt in the world, although other songs, such as "Nancy," stress despair and death. And while most of the songs are of normal duration, "Please Don't Pass Me By (A Disgrace)," taped from the 1970 Royal Albert Hall concert, plays for thirteen minutes and fifty-five seconds, Cohen's longest recorded song ("Death of a Ladies' Man" at nine minutes and twenty seconds and "Always" at eight minutes and two seconds are his second and third longest recordings.) But the sense of isolation during this period of his life remains throughout the album; a line from "Passing Thru" makes this sense clear: "I'm an orphan now and I'm only passing through. So are you!"

In order to escape some of the domestic and personal turmoil of living with Suzanne Elrod, Cohen returned to Israel in September 1973 for two months of duty, touring military bases and entertaining the soldiers engaged in the ongoing conflict with Egypt, which erupted into the Yom Kippur War of October 1973. He was posted to the support-services branch and sang for the troops at various bases during the anxious period preceding the war. The song "Lover Lover Lover," written in the Sinai and recorded on *New Skin for the Old Ceremony*, grew out of this experience. Returning to Canada, Cohen hosted Bob Dylan and his Canadian girlfriend for several weeks.

Trying to deal with the uneven emotions generated by the turmoil of his personal life, Cohen began a fourth novel, which, like his first — "Ballet of Lepers" — remains unpublished. Recorded in his notebooks, it is massive — including poems, journal entries, and prose passages — and tentatively entitled "The Woman Being Born," also an alternate title for "My Life in Art," which appears as a section in Cohen's 1978 work, *Death of a Lady's Man* (MacSkimming, " 'New' Leonard Cohen"). In 1973 Cohen had also completed a draft of a new book of poems tentatively called "Notes for the Clean Life," which may be an early version of "The Woman Being Born" (Kapica; Ruhlmann 19).

Cohen released his fifth album, *New Skin for the Old Ceremony*, in 1974, its military character the result of songs of obedience and bravery, enemies and friends, courage and fear. "Field Commander Cohen," outlining the supposed authority of the commander, is a parodic example. Critics thought the album more successful than its predecessors because its songs were more reflective and better produced. An effort at a richer sound was apparent, with broader musical accompaniment than on earlier records, although Cohen still felt that there was plenty of "hurt" on the album, for he was "learning how to sing again" (qtd. in Dorman 271).

Forgiveness and reconciliation are themes on the album, yet frustration rings every verse, beginning with the opening song, "Is This What You Wanted?" This song about the constant searching for union between male and female is opposed by "Chelsea Hotel #2," which narrates the affair of two lovers at the New York headquarters of the music scene in the seventies. A tribute to Janis Joplin, it records an important, shared passage for both singers. In "Lover Lover Lover," Cohen blames his betrayal of his Jewishness as the cause of the breakup of his family life and seeks to change his name from the priestly Kohen to another, less demanding one: he seeks "a face that's fair this time; I want a spirit that is calm." Yet what the remainder of the album stresses is that life is worth something only if it is lived honestly. "There Is a War" reiterates this view through the battle between what his lover seeks and what he knows to be wrong, because she cannot stand what he is trying to become in order to be true to himself. "A singer must die for the lie in his voice,"

Cohen declares in "A Singer Must Die," his effort to renounce dishonesty. "Take This Longing," a rewrite of his early song "The Bells," expresses his deep desire to unite the bodily with the spiritual. The concluding song, "Leaving Greensleeves," thematizes rejected love and departure, the lover leaving because he can suffer no longer, although he admits that telling lies was the only way he thought he could achieve her love. He was wrong.

Coinciding with the album was an off-Broadway play produced by Cohen's New York lawyer, Marty Machat. Entitled *Sisters of Mercy*, the production, which had previewed at the Shaw Festival in the summer of 1973, opened in New York on 25 September 1973 to a middling reception. Clive Barnes of the *New York Times* summarized the plot as a record of the loves of a dissolute Montreal poet whom women found irresistible, although this young Bohemian is at heart merely a little boy. Despite the actors' enthusiasm, the play was not a success.

The London release of Cohen's film *Bird on the Wire* shortly after his album *New Skin for the Old Ceremony* was, however, a hit. Revising the original version, which cost over $100,000 to produce, Cohen spent six months in England editing and rearranging the film to show the deeper elements of his music, the conditions that produced it, and his interaction with audiences. It contains songs from albums as well as concerts, including those in Berlin, Vienna, Copenhagen, and Israel in March and April 1972. A documentary rather than art film, the work found an appreciative audience as Cohen began his third and longest European tour, performing thirty-three concerts in fifty days, from 1 September to 19 October 1974. Spain was a major stop, and in Barcelona he dedicated the concert to Lorca and his influence on his own work. One result of Cohen's popularity there was the immediate translation of his work into Spanish.

On his return to North America, Cohen was asked to join Earl Scruggs for a recording session, which took place in Nashville in late 1974. The song was a cover of Cohen's "Passing Thru" from *Live Songs* (1973); the musicians included Earl Scruggs on banjo and Billy Joel on piano, with backup vocals by Joan Baez, Buffy Sainte-Marie, Ramblin' Jack Elliott, and The Pointer Sisters. A few concerts followed, beginning in November 1974 with two nights at the Bottom Line in New York and continuing in Toronto at Massey Hall on 31 January 1975, Philadelphia in early February, and New York again, this time at Avery Fisher Hall on 7 February. Always enjoying the performances, Cohen and his group averaged a remarkable twenty-six songs each concert.

However, at the end of this minitour, he again became despondent over his deteriorating domestic situation. He withdrew to his hillside home in Hydra for most of 1975 as he sought to reconnect with his family. His "disappearance" was so marked that, at his early December 1975 Rolling Thunder Revue concert in Montreal, Bob Dylan, in what many believe has been one of his finest performances, dedicated his song "Isis" to Cohen (who was backstage) with these words: "This is for Leonard, if he's still here!" (qtd. in Dorman 282).

At this time, however, arrangements for guitar and voice appeared in another Amsco publication, *New Skin for the Old Ceremony* (1975), which includes reviews of the 1974 album reprinted from *Crawdaddy* and *Rolling Stone*. But this success again brought disillusionment, and Cohen retreated to reassess his goals. The "angry young ironist," as a critic in London described him (qtd. in Dorman 282), was reexamining his intentions, describing the process in language that would become the basis of his next book, *Death of a Lady's Man*, his first in six years. "I Knelt beside a Stream," the opening prose poem, initiates his revolt against what he calls "the obscene silence of my career as a lady's man" (11). "I am grumpy," he later writes in *"The Rebellion,"* "because I cannot indicate the vastness of my heart" (163). "Blackening pages" — his term for writing and composing, first used in *The Favorite Game* (177) — became his salvation, his means of confronting and working out the dilemma between his need to recover his identity and, yet, not to sacrifice his family. Through frequent meditation and reconsideration, he sought ways to combat his need to free his soul and his art, expressed in

"The Idols of the Lord" in the polarity between unity and separation:

> Divide my world
> from skin to core
> or make it one
> as it was before. (135)

Seeking to capitalize on Cohen's reputation, CBS records released *The Best of Leonard Cohen* in 1975. The album, entitled *Leonard Cohen's Greatest Hits* in England, includes twelve songs: "Suzanne," "Sisters of Mercy," "Bird on the Wire," "The Partisan," "Famous Blue Raincoat," and "Take This Longing," plus six others. Commercially successful, especially in Europe, it nevertheless did not receive critical praise. However, Cohen soon began his fourth European tour, a lengthy fifty-five-concert journey over seventy-eight days, beginning in Berlin in late April 1976 and ending in London in early July. Düsseldorf, Dublin, Oslo, Oxford, and Zurich were stops. Tapings of these concerts were frequently broadcast, thus allowing Cohen to reach wider and wider audiences of differing ages. Indeed, his reputation grew to such proportions that someone apparently took to impersonating him on one of the Greek islands in order to seduce female tourists.

The end of this European tour brought Cohen face to face with the reality of his doomed relationship with Suzanne, generated in part by the shattering pull of his need for inner peace in the face of constant domestic turmoil. He returned to Los Angeles and shared accommodations with several fellow students of Zen master Joshu Sasaki. He resurrected his unpublished manuscript "My Life in Art," disrupting sequences and generalizing statements about his life as a lady's man, although this process failed to diminish his antagonism and bitterness. The Garden of Eden, as well as the battle of Armageddon, formulate the text.

Dedicated to Cohen's mother, who died of leukemia in 1978 — the only previous texts with this dedication were British and

FIGURE 14

The cover of The Best of Leonard Cohen, *released in 1975.*

Canadian editions of *The Favorite Game* — *Death of a Lady's Man* (1978) has as its cover a gold-embossed image of a sixteenth-century symbolic representation of the *coniunctio spirituum*, or the "spiritual union," of the male and female principles, also used on the cover of the 1974 album *New Skin for the Old Ceremony*. The source is an alchemical text, *Rosararium Philosophorum*, a book that Cohen first located in California through Carl Jung's *Psychology and Alchemy* (1953). Interestingly, the image idealizes the union of male and female figures, no longer possible for Cohen at this time. Not since his use in *Beautiful Losers* of the 1927 account of Catherine Tekakwitha by a French Jesuit has a specialized text expressed so many of the ideas and themes in a work that concentrates on sacrifice and suffering.

Death of a Lady's Man, completed but withdrawn in proof from the publisher, was preceded by Cohen's sixth album, *Death of a Ladies' Man* (1977). The plural designation suggests a wider application of this death, one caused by many women, but also the possibility of a broader renewal. The album was recorded by Los Angeles rock producer Phil Spector, whose meteoric rise began with the 1958 hit, "To Know Him Is To Love Him." The "wall of sound" and the extended use of echoes became Spector trademarks. Cohen's lawyer Marty Machat introduced the two, and Cohen at first looked forward to their collaboration in an effort to realize a pop album and alter his sound. But their working relationship proved to be difficult at best, uncompromising at worst, as Cohen lost control of the sound and even of the lyrics. He has, nevertheless, referred to the album as "a grotesque masterpiece. Spector's a mad genius, but he *is* a genius," he said in 1980 (qtd. in Godfrey). On the album, the songs are listed as "by Spector & Cohen," even those previously published as poems. Cohen had hoped to find Spector in his Debussyan period but found him in a state of Wagnerian tumult.

The eight songs on the album range from the mordant "True Love Leaves No Traces" to the sensational "Don't Go Home with Your Hard-On," the latter using Bob Dylan and Allen Ginsberg as backup vocalists. This arrangement came about by accident: one night while eating with Ronee Blakely at Cantor's Delicatessen on Fairfax Avenue in Los Angeles, Dylan and Ginsberg had learned that Cohen was recording with Spector. They had gone over, and Spector, in a dictatorial mood, had ordered them to join in on the backup vocals.

The title song displays elements of female rather than male chauvinism, the women finding the man in distress, taking him, using and losing him, emasculating him. Mention of St. Francis of Assisi refers to an aborted project to write the score for a movie about the saint proposed by Franco Zeffirelli; apparently, the project had fallen apart when Cohen suggested that everyone work for free, in the spirit of the saint. The song and the album conclude with emptiness, with the repetitive, trailing sound of "I guess you go for nothing / if you really want to go that far." At this time, Cohen's self-delusion was complete. His personal life was crumbling with the breakup of his marriage, and his mother's life was ending. In order to be with her, Cohen moved his family back to Montreal. Her death in 1978 created a tremendous gap in his life.

Death of a Lady's Man, the book, followed the album. Its 216 pages mix poetry with journal entries expressing the lyrical, dramatic, and musical. Persistent themes such as sexual self-pity, betrayal, and masochistic revelation shape the text. The violation of solemn contracts — expressed through self-deprecation and mystical invocation, the use of magic and religious ceremony, what Eli Mandel has disingenuously labelled, in "Leonard Cohen's Brilliant Con Game," "Zen Judaism" (52), and remarkable inventiveness — creates an absorbing book that is something of a summa of Cohen's life to 1977. Suddenly, popular culture and the apocalypse had united.

In many ways *Death of a Lady's Man* is the most postmodern work of Canadian poetry published in the seventies: it challenges its romantic self-awareness with a postmodern intertextuality. Through its textual play of drafts, versions, commentaries, and supposedly completed poems, with its supplementary use of journal entries, commentators, sources, and dialogues, one discovers a work in the tradition of the process poem. Many of the commentaries provide information about the genesis of the poems; others provide original versions of the works, with their records self-consciously identified, as in the notebook that Cohen had purchased from a stationer on Wardour Street in London in the winter of 1972 (96). Other sections consist of parts of the first draft of the book or his final revisions to "My Life in Art." Yet revision itself becomes a metaphor for the process of interpretation because his commentaries, often sharing the same title as the original text, revise or analyse the first statement. The postmodern self-awareness contributes to the tangled dimension of the work, an adjunct and extension of the album *Death of a Ladies' Man*.

Interspersed with the prose-poem journals in *Death of a Lady's Man* are flashes of lyricism, which have often been the most seductive aspect of Cohen's work. "Now I Come before You" and *"The Rose"* are two examples, the latter possessing an amusingly ironic rejection of paradise:

> I miss the vice of a man like Christ
> And there's too many Arthur Rimbauds
> But I'm not going back to Paradise
> And I'm not going back to The Rose. (121)

Surrealism overpowers the text, leaving readers searching for a centre. Instead of structural changes in the poems, Cohen provides only a modulation of tone. Yet underlying all is an acknowledgement of the terror of the times; or, as he writes in "How to Speak Poetry," "There is nothing you can show on your face that can match the horror of this time" (196). Consequently, one must "Respect the privacy of the material," of the words; "The poem is not a slogan. It cannot advertise you" (197).

Death of a Lady's Man is a metafictional work, the culmination of the formal self-reflexiveness in *Beautiful Losers*. Focusing on the failure of his marriage to the unfaithful woman of the title, Cohen makes it clear that sexual relations condition literary realities, but lies are everywhere, textually as well as morally: *"There is no death in this book and therefore it is a lie,"* he states in *"She Has Given Me the Bullet"* (113). Yet this cross between a novel and a collection of poetic meditations, his version of the *I Ching* that he had wanted to write, clears the way for the restoration of the self in his 1984 collection of psalms, *Book of Mercy.*

RENEWAL AND REASSESSMENT

By the late seventies, Cohen was alone: his companion had left; his mother had died. Only time spent with his Zen master in California seemed to heal the hurt. The *zendo* training was not an end in itself but a preparation for a furthering of the self. Cohen became more involved in the operation of the Buddhist centre, developing a strong friendship with Roshi. He also concentrated on his physical development, working out at a YMCA not far from his home. By 1978, he had an immense following in Europe, where his book sales were estimated to be two million and his record sales ten million. His personal renewal occurred gradually, as reflected in his 1979 album *Recent Songs*, released only two years after *Death of a Ladies' Man.*

Reworking his Jewish, Zen, and artistic traditions, Cohen produced an album rich in traditional sounds despite its title. He dedicated it to Irving Layton, "My friend and inspiration, the incomparable expert of interior language," and acknowledged that its true producer was his late mother, Masha Cohen. Critics liked the album for its rescue of "real passionate romance" (qtd. in Dorman 299), and the *New York Times* listed it among the top ten albums of 1979. Recorded in Los Angeles, it is Cohen's best album of the period, for he had sought a sound that would rediscover the sources and harmonies of his earlier work. Joining him were Jennifer Warnes as a backup vocalist, Steve Meador on drums, and Paul Ostermayer on saxophone; the latter two were part of the 1993 world tour. Members of an Austin, Texas, jazz group, Passenger, also assisted.

Thematically, the ten songs on the album range from the mystical to the realistic, although the religious constantly unites the intimate and the epic. The sacred and the secular intertwine in the opening song, "The Guests," which sets the welcoming and inclusive tone. Cohen does not propose a simple recovery, but is aware of a new path, as "Humbled in Love" outlines and "The Window" summarizes in its encomium to the lover: "O darling of angels, demons and saints, / And the whole broken-hearted host: / Gentle this soul." Revenge and retribution have been replaced by awareness of a higher love. "The Traitor," "Our Lady of Solitude," and "The Gypsy's Wife" —- the last borrow-ing from Lorca's powerful play, *Blood Wedding*—express not only Cohen's sorrow over Suzanne's departure (she had moved from Los Angeles to Aix-en-Provence) but also his tentative steps toward recovery. Conciliation emerges more strongly than hate, although Cohen realizes that he cannot return to a former state of union with her. "Ballad of the Absent Mare," ostensibly about an escaped horse, is also an allegorical expression of the missing love that has caused his life to collapse through the "panic of loss"; art, however, provides the way to recovery.

Both *The Energy of Slaves* and *Death of a Lady's Man* had received hostile reviews, partly because of their negative tone and spiteful, if not hateful, poses. But to set the image of Cohen in his aggressive phase (recall the picture of the poet as rebel on the jacket of *The Energy of Slaves*) against that of his self-revisionary phase (note again the image of the uniting angels on the cover of *Death of a Lady's Man*) is to understand that he was working slowly toward renewal, which *Recent Songs* affirms. It replaces the anticelebration of *New Skin for the Old Ceremony* and *Death of a Ladies' Man* with an inclusive spirituality poised between the sacred and the real. Dismissed as a serious writer after the appearance of his two negatively reviewed books, Cohen turned to song in his search for salvation, although his deracinated self established the tenor of his singing, with pain overpowering love and his presentation of women becoming allegories of his existence.

Cohen undertook another tour of Europe following the release of *Recent Songs*. Beginning in October and ending in mid-December 1979, it took him to forty-six cities. Rehearsing first in London, he then visited the usual countries: England, Denmark, Norway, Sweden, France, Germany, and Switzerland, ending the sixty-nine-day tour in Brighton, England. Accompanying him for a good portion of the journey was Harry Rasky, the Canadian documentary filmmaker, who prepared *The Song of Leonard Cohen* for CBC Television release in 1980. The tour was demanding: Cohen explained to a journalist that "Everybody on tour has had a tiny nervous breakdown at one point or the other. I don't know if it's the weather, or the tour's intensity, or the music. . . . They just carry our bodies from hotel room to airport bus, and the music manifests itself each night" (qtd. in Dorman 310). Seriousness became his trademark, which European fans found genuine if not compelling. But, as he explained to Stephen Godfrey of the *Globe and Mail*, he found the market for his singing more receptive in Europe than in North America: "I find I get more support from the record companies in Europe. Here, the emphasis is on the quick hit. They're not concerned about an artist's past work."

A tour of Australia followed the release of an expensive *livre d'artiste* of seven poems. Spending two weeks at the Buddhist monastery before his departure, Cohen refined his meditative outlook, which the concerts embodied. From Sydney to Melbourne, he performed before packed houses and received constant praise in the press. He performed rock, folk, jazz, and spiritual music, as well as new, unrecorded songs, before a wildly enthusiastic public. The *Sydney Mirror* referred to him as "the music renaissance man," while the *Sydney Morning Herald* called him "the darling of the thinking flower-children" (qtd. in Dorman 315).

In late October 1980, Cohen began his sixth tour of Europe, adding several concerts in Israel. Germany, where he had developed an immense following, was one of his most popular stops. After performing in Berlin, Hamburg, and Freiburg, he and his group flew to Tel Aviv.

After the tour, he settled again in his hilltop home in Hydra and experimented with the song cycle and the Spenserian stanza (eight five-foot iambic lines, followed by an iambic line of six feet, rhyming ababbcbcc). Montreal friend and musician Lewis Furey was with him, and, in the winter of 1981, they began a pop opera about a rock star who becomes burnt out. *Night Magic* was the title. The Spanish writer Alberto Manzano was researching his account of Cohen at this time, staying with him on Hydra and witnessing Cohen's enjoyment in being both a father to his two children and an active composer. Jewish food, records such as *Hymns of the Temple*, music by Bach and by the contemporary pianist Keith Jarrett, a friend from the Newport Festival days — all were there. And in North America, Cohen's acclaim was growing — not only through the various critical studies of his work that had begun to appear in the late seventies but also through another off-Broadway production entitled *Bird on the Wire*, which premièred at the American Arts Festival.

Embodying this period of reassessment, roughly from 1980 to 1984, is *Book of Mercy*, which coincided with Cohen's removal from the public spotlight for several years as he shifted from Hydra to New York, Montreal, and then Los Angeles. Its release in 1984 was a risk because it displays a further and publicly unexpected shift into prayer, mysticism, and religion — a shift away from the lyrical or dramatic that had dominated his work in the seventies. Yet, as with its predecessor, Cohen experimented by selecting the prose poem as its form, the fifty psalms paralleling his fifty years. The work further confirms Cohen's progress from death to resurrection, from the despair of *Death of a Lady's Man* to the spiritual renewal of *Book of Mercy*, the 1979 album *Recent Songs* being a stage along the way.

The cover design of *Book of Mercy* uses a symbol that Cohen drew: two intertwined hearts evoking the Star of David. An emotional hexagram with the rough edges rounded, it has become his symbol for his "Order of the Unified Heart," offered to guests and friends as a lapel pin. But this order has no meetings, bylaws, or dues (Wieseltier 44). Of course, as a subject,

FIGURE 15

*Publicity shot of Cohen working in
Los Angeles in 1983 at desk with guitar.*

mercy has long been present in his work, in both his poetry and song: "Sisters of Mercy," from his first album, and "The Story of Isaac," from his second, are two early examples; "The Law," from his ninth album, *Various Positions*, continues the theme. At first called "A Book of Psalms," *Book of Mercy* is a prayer, confession, and apologia. It praises psalms as a means of personal fulfilment, as the twenty-eighth psalm states: "Arouse my heart again with the limitless breath you breath into me, arouse the secret from obscurity" (n. pag.). The origin of the book was actually in silence, according to Cohen: "I was silenced in all areas. I couldn't move. I was up against the wall. It was the only way I could penetrate through my predicament." What happened next, he told Alan Twigg, was his discovery of "the courage to write down my prayers. To apply to the source of mercy. . . . I found that the act of writing was the proper form for my prayer" ("Leonard Cohen" 45, 46). But he has found it a difficult book to discuss because prayer in this age is so out of place: "We're such a hip age. Nobody wants to affirm those realities. It doesn't go with your sunglasses" (46). Nevertheless, he indicated to Doug Fetherling the paradox that those uninterested in writing might find the book more appealing than those interested in writing:

> there would be certain agreements that would be unchallenged, unquestioned by ordinary church-going people who have not been exposed to modern writing and would have no relationship to anything Joycean or post-Joycean — and I also think that people who have too deep an investment in modernism would find the book offensive from that point of view. ("Leonard Cohen" 30)

Conscious of its traditional, biblical roots, Cohen anticipated the criticism that the book is conservative and derivative — and too religious. Not surprisingly, at the period of its composition, Cohen had become a more devout Jew, regularly attending synagogue.

Book of Mercy is possibly Cohen's most characteristic text because it transposes the language of prayer and ritual for that of contemporary experience in order to articulate a spiritual and moral renewal. It literally compares the mythologies that he began to explore in 1956. The book is a set of prayers that exposes the speaker's weakness, sorrow, and guilt as he confronts what at first appears to be an incomprehensible universe. The poetic psalms grew out of three or four years of introspection and took Cohen approximately eighteen months to complete in 1982–83. The genre is a blend of Old Testament style with New Testament themes, summarized, aesthetically as well as spiritually, by Psalms 4.1: "HEAR me when I call, O God of my righteousness: thou hast enlarged me *when I was* in distress; have mercy upon me, and hear my prayer" (KJV). This plea is that of the speaker throughout Cohen's book.

Book of Mercy represents the recovery and soaring of the spirit that had been undone by loss and suffering. It anticipates a line from Cohen's soon-to-be-released 1985 album *Various Positions*, on which a verse from the song "Hallelujah" reads, "I heard there was a secret chord / that David played to please the Lord." Cohen discovers this chord in his psalms, but such a discovery involves servitude. The intensity of searching unmasks him, creating a work more open and exposed than any of his previous texts. The result is a piety of strength, an awareness that he is living below what is above, powerfully expressed by Cohen but not easily accessed by casual readers. The inability of many readers to respond seems to have proven Cohen's point about the divorce of the spiritual from the mundane. In some ways he had anticipated this difficulty, expecting few readers to identify with his prayers. Reviewers were mixed in their assessment, although the book did win the 1985 Canadian Authors' Association Literary Award for Poetry.

A book of prayer, a book of prophecy, a book of mercy. Cohen's work is a coda of his previous texts, all steps on a journey to recover the soul through the trials of life and experience what his poetry often expresses: "Serve the LORD with fear, and rejoice

FIGURE 16

*Cohen and Irving Layton at a 1984 book signing
for* Book of Mercy *and Layton's* Final Reckoning.

with trembling" (Psalms 2.11, KJV). In many ways a romantic return to an unblemished origin of purity, the speaker's quest parallels that of David in The Book of Psalms, Dante in the *Divine Comedy*, or Pilgrim in *Pilgrim's Progress*. In praise about, in anguish over, and in conflict with the events of his life, Cohen constructs a book of private meditations that seem inviolate, making readers who enter them seem rude. But for those who do, it is also a book of hope; the thirty-first psalm states: "Your name is the sweetness of time, and you carry me close into the night, speaking consolations, . . . saying, See how the night has no terror for one who remembers the Name" (n. pag.). This book of devotions, similar to those of seventeenth-century divines, remains a singular work, which, while differing in form from earlier publications, is the culmination of Cohen's many themes and concerns, with a discipline not seen in his earlier poetry.

The year after *Book of Mercy* appeared, Cohen released a new album, *Various Positions* (available in late 1984 in Europe, it appeared in North America in 1985); it also provides a set of ritual offerings to listeners, although with a sensuality richer than on *Recent Songs*. The album marked a new direction in his music; breaking away from the Spector-induced drive to create a big pop sound, and adding depth to his earlier arrangements, Cohen created a deeper, more engaging sound. He drew increasingly on electronic instruments and studio technology, which actually isolate his deep voice from intrusive instruments; this technique has carried through to his two subsequent and successful albums, *I'm Your Man* and *The Future*. But Cohen's not having sung in North America since the Bread and Roses festival in Berkeley in 1980, and with the disappointing sales of *Death of a Ladies' Man* and *Recent Songs*, CBS, Cohen's major record company, refused to distribute *Various Positions* in the United States, although CBS in Canada and Europe did so under the company name. Cohen learned of this decision accidentally in Europe when an American record executive could not find an American release date. The president of Columbia Records sharply outlined the problem when he said, "Leonard, we know you're great, but we don't know if you're any good" (qtd. in Ruhlmann 20). The Passport Label of little-known Jem Records finally distributed the album in the United States, although it released a very limited supply. Two songs on the record focus on psalms: "If It Be Your Will," a prayer for the serenity brought by obedience, and a hymn in an upbeat, modern arrangement entitled "Hallelujah." The album renews the complexities of a typical Cohen song, as in "The Law" or "The Captain," but not at the expense of musicality or melody. "Dance Me to the End of Love," the opening song, evokes a powerful love inspired by the horrific incongruity of classical music performed next to the crematoria in the concentration camps. A modest commercial success, the album reached number fifty-two on the United Kingdom charts; in Scandinavia, Spain, and Portugal, it garnered top ratings; elsewhere, though, sales were not strong. More importantly, it marks the emergence of a clearer artistic purpose and a new sense of aesthetic wholeness following the catharsis of *Book of Mercy*.

In the spring of 1983, preceding the release of both *Book of Mercy* and *Various Positions*, Cohen made a video entitled *I Am a Hotel*, with Anne Ditchburn, a noted choreographer, providing the dance sequences. Five songs became the musical score: "Memories," "The Guests," "The Gypsy's Wife," "Chelsea Hotel #2," and "Suzanne." The concept was based on the reminiscences of a hotel — or at least of certain rooms in the hotel. Filmed at the King Edward Hotel in Toronto, the five scenarios project links between the residents of the hotel and the songs of Cohen, who appears intermittently in the video. Moses Znaimer, a long-time friend and president of CITY TV in Toronto (and who later presided over Cohen's induction into the Juno Hall of Fame in March 1991), and Barrie Wexler joined Cohen in forming the Blue Memorial Video company to make the film. So successful was the video that it won first prize at an international television festival in Montreux, Switzerland, and had prime-time showing in North America and Europe in 1984.

Cohen's creativity went further when he completed an opera

with Lewis Furey, variously entitled "Merry-Go Man," *Night Magic* (the title used at its debut in Cannes), "The Hall," and "Angel Eyes." Cohen had begun the libretto on Hydra in 1981; Furey had composed the music and later directed the cast. Cohen thought of it as a ballet, Furey an opera, and it thus became a musical pastiche. Neither actor Nick Mancuso nor dancers Frank Augustyn and Anik Bissonette could eliminate the basic fragmentariness of the work. Yet it marked Cohen's reentry into the musical world after nearly a five-year absence (1979–84), a reentry capped by his winning a Juno Award in 1985 for Best Movie Score for his contribution to this "rock opera." His career quickly accelerated with new tours and new albums more popular than ever.

The eighties became the comeback years for Cohen. The musical and poetic confusions of the seventies resulted in the painful rediscovery of his traditions, culminating in the prose poems of *Book of Mercy* and the spirituality of *Various Positions*. He was slowly moving away from the status of cult hero and European wonder into the mainstream North American market. A new tour, which began on 31 January 1985 in Mannheim, carried Cohen not only throughout Germany, Scandinavia, Spain, France, England, and Austria but also, for the first time, to Poland, where he discovered an annual Leonard Cohen Festival occurring in Kraków. Forty-two concerts later, he triumphantly returned to North America, where some audiences, such as those in New York, had not seen him perform for ten years.

In April he began a North American tour in Philadelphia, prefaced by an interview on WNEW-FM in New York, during which he read several poems. The tour took him to Boston and then to Carnegie Hall in New York, Massey Hall in Toronto, Place des Arts in Montreal, and the Queen Elizabeth Theatre in Vancouver. From there he went to Brisbane, Sydney, Melbourne, Adelaide, and Perth. He returned to play in San Francisco and then at the Wiltern Theatre in Los Angeles, where, at the 9 June 1985 performance, Bob Dylan, Joni Mitchell, and Al Kooper joined him backstage. Indefatigably, he went on to Europe for

FIGURE 17

Cohen at the South Monica Pier in beret with cigarette in 1985.

several extra concerts and continued on to Israel. Playing in Jerusalem and Caesarea, he was not well received, one critic reporting that Cohen had "grown out of his songs" (qtd. in Dorman 351). He then visited Austria, Switzerland, Spain, and finally southern France, completing his tour in Saint-Jean-de-Luz.

At the end of nearly six months of touring (including his first swing through Europe), Cohen returned to the nondescript Royalton Hotel at 44 West 44th Street in New York, where he had been living before the tour in order to be near his children. Appearances on *Saturday Night Live*, and readings from March through May 1986, broadened his exposure and appeal, and he enjoyed a triumph at New York's Carnival of the Spoken Word, which also featured Allen Ginsberg.

In late 1986, Cohen achieved a new dimension of fame when Jennifer Warnes released her cover album, *Famous Blue Raincoat*. Cohen and Warnes had, of course, known each other for years. Singing on the 1972 and 1979 tours, she had become one of his principal backup singers, adding a lilting voice to offset his gravelly croak. When she decided to record her cover album, she chose arrangements that feature the upbeat sound of contemporary music and invited Cohen to sing on "Joan of Arc," which they recorded in March 1986 at The Complex in Los Angeles. To assist Warnes in producing the album, Cohen moved back to Los Angeles for four months and reworked several songs. He also aided in the making of her video for "First We Take Manhattan," and it was on the set in a Los Angeles warehouse that Sharon Weisz took the candid shot of Cohen eating a banana; the photo later became the album cover for *I'm Your Man* and the signature image for his 1988 tour.

Critical acclaim and commercial gain greeted the release of *Famous Blue Raincoat*, which thrust Cohen into the musical spotlight again. The album reached number eight in the United States, was listed for seven weeks in a top spot in England, and went gold in Canada. Worldwide, the album sold over 750,000 copies and was largely responsible for reintroducing Cohen to North American audiences. Or, as one critic quipped, Warnes made Cohen's voice respectable again in America. From a rhyth-mic "First We Take Manhattan" to a pulsating "Bird on a Wire," Warnes reinterpreted Cohen for a new and welcoming audience.

TOWER OF SONG

In Los Angeles Cohen worked on a new album, although it was actually recorded in Montreal and Los Angeles, with one song, "Take This Waltz," taped in Paris. Warnes contributed backup vocals and assistance in arranging the songs. The result was an album of towering success, unified in conception, which the title, *I'm Your Man*, strikingly and directly expresses. The album, Cohen's tenth, is not a platform for his views but a manifestation of himself. Released in England on 14 February 1988, and later in the United States and Canada, it quickly took off, being nomi-nated for best album of the year in both Great Britain and the United States. It sold one million copies in Europe and went gold in Canada. For seventeen weeks it was number one in Norway, where it went platinum, and it also topped the charts in Spain. And that year it won for Cohen the coveted Crystal Globe award from CBS Records, an award reserved for its outstanding perform-ers. Cohen accepted it with the improvised remark, "I have always been touched by the modesty of their interest in my work." The album's secular and confident tone gave it a quality unmatched by any of his previous recordings. Spurning the public's view of him as a depressing writer, Cohen concentrated on his art and personal expression. Appearing at a time when punk, heavy metal, and glossy pop music were losing their appeal, *I'm Your Man* provided a beat, a message, and a voice that were captivating.

Dedicated to Dominique Issermann, a French photographer, the album begins with the up-tempo "First We Take Manhat-tan," which Warnes had recorded. The song is a critique of modern culture and a signal of personal power to fight the corrosive institutions of fashion and music. It is a challenging but convincingly presented sound. "Ain't No Cure for Love" follows, its focus on the private heart. It is also a journey, but one of loss, as Cohen stated: it "Started from the heart of man and (proceeded) to the heart of God, but the ladder's been removed. And there ain't no band-aid big enough to cover up this wound" (qtd. in Dorman 359). Yet the love is everlasting and everpresent, and it requires no repentance: "I don't need to be forgiven for loving you so much. It's written in the scriptures. It's written there in blood. I even heard the angels declare it from above. There ain't no cure for love."

All the archetypes are dissolving, Cohen remarked at the time of the album's release, underscoring the need to redefine them. So people return to their pasts to forgive those who betray them, to believe in love, to recognize that their independence is their strength. "I'm Your Man" emphasizes this return, as does the wonderfully evocative song "I Can't Forget," which in melody and rhythm returns one convincingly to a haunting country-and-western sound, which Cohen has long admired. "Take This Waltz" rewrites Lorca and enters a different musical syntax on the album, while the enigmatic "Jazz Police" represents jazz fusion and an Orwellian world of persecution. "Tower of Song," the concluding number, is a riveting set of images in a haunting melody that navigates between desire and aging. It contains two classic Cohen statements: the opening refrain — "Well, my friends are gone and my hair is grey. I ache in the places where I used to play. And I'm crazy for love but I'm not coming on. I'm just paying my rent everyday in the Tower of Song" — and the seriocomic line, "I was born like this, I had no choice. I was born with the gift of a golden voice." But print does not convey the excellence of Cohen's voice, and the delivery of this song, on the album.

The record's success prompted a sixty-five-concert, worldwide tour. It started in Frankfurt and ended sixty-one days later in Dublin (on 4 June 1988). In April Columbia released a single of "Ain't No Cure for Love"; to aid its promotion and that of the tour, Cohen sent a personal letter to Columbia sales represen-

FIGURE 18

Cohen performing in Mannheim,
Germany, on 4 December 1988.

tatives, enclosing two dollars in each envelope to encourage the album's distribution. In Iceland he was received by its president and in England by Prince Charles. Over twenty people accompanied him on the tour, including six musicians, sound crew, road crew, backup singers, tour manager, and musical director. Merchandise included T-shirts, sweatshirts, programs, and even limited editions of Cohen's watercolour paintings. In the maelstrom of the tour, Cohen nevertheless remained stoic, disciplined, and in control because of new inner peace as well as worldly success. Mixing meditation with musical composition, press conferences, interviews, sound checks, and performances, Cohen found the tour an engaging preoccupation of work and musical refinement. And nearly two hours before every concert, he would retire to regain his inner composure and equilibrium, which he frequently managed to project to his audience, the concerts becoming acts of communion rather than performances.

After the tour, Cohen soon adopted a private life that saw him write, spend time in Paris with his children, and shuttle between Montreal, New York, Los Angeles, and, when time permitted, Hydra. But new attention greeted him: a guest appearance on *Austin City Limits* met with great success, and he also appeared in the film *A Moving Picture* (he had also performed in a 1986 episode of *Miami Vice*, playing the head of Interpol). Other acknowledgements included his being voted one of the "10 Sexiest Men" in Canada by *Chatelaine* and honoured by the Performing Rights Organization of Canada. Cohen expressed the maturity of his career in a 1987 interview with the London magazine *Time Out*, stressing that a new strength joined his vulnerability, what he characterized as "the true experiences of a 53-year-old with no subtractions" (qtd. in Dorman 373). One of these "experiences" was an unreleased album of recitations from *Book of Mercy*, set to a string quartet conducted by Jeremy Lubbock.

But as new songs needed to be written, Cohen's life took new directions. Living in Montreal and Los Angeles, he began working on a magnum opus, "Democracy," which the 1992 album *The*

FIGURE 19

Cohen at a press conference in Frankfurt, Germany, in 1988.

Future distills from eighty verses to six. Occasionally in interviews, such as the one with Peter Gzowski on the popular CBC Radio show *Morningside* of 18 November 1992, Cohen has cited unused verses from the song. One of them is:

It ain't comin' to us European-style,
Concentration camp behind the smile;
It ain't comin' from the east
With its temporary feast
As Count Dracula comes strolling down the aisle.

The song took Cohen nearly three years to complete, although he had to interrupt work on the original to nurse his son Adam back from a near-fatal 1990 road accident in Guadeloupe, spending nearly four months in a North York, Ontario, hotel while visiting him daily. Afterward, Cohen found it hard to reengage with the original project: "There was the normal, dismal process of assembling and rejecting, medication, heavy drinking, giving up smoking, changing girlfriends, y'know . . . all the stuff that goes into these things," Cohen said, referring to the hiatus (qtd. in Jackson). Yet he found the need to create inescapable and returned to a series of important new songs, some of which he had started years before.

Cohen's earlier songs continued to be popular, and the Neville Brothers recorded a top-ten hit with "Bird on a Wire" in 1990, the year that Mel Gibson and Goldie Hawn starred in a mediocre feature film of the same title. Two other songs, "Everybody Knows" and "If It Be Your Will," were used in the moderately successful teen movie, *Pump Up the Volume* (released in August 1990), starring Christian Slater. Concrete Blonde sang the cover version of "Everybody Knows" for part of the soundtrack for this movie about an underground teenage disc jockey in Arizona.

In September 1991, Cohen's popularity reached international proportions with a new generation when the tribute album *I'm Your Fan* appeared. Initiated by Christian Fevret, editor of the largest-selling rock magazine in France, *Les inrockuptibles*, it features work by House of Love, Ian McCulloch, The Pixies, Nick Cave, REM, and John Cale. The cover songs include "Hey, That's No Way to Say Goodbye," "I Can't Forget," "Suzanne," "First We Take Manhattan," "Chelsea Hotel #2," "Tower of Song," and "Hallelujah." Public-relations material for the album describes Cohen's songs as combining "simple melodic arrangements with deeply confessional lyrics." More importantly, the groups on the album have all been influenced by Cohen's sound and words, and the recording was meant to introduce his work to a younger generation of fans "who might think he was too old for them."

Earlier, on 3 March 1991 in Vancouver, Cohen was inducted into the Juno Hall of Fame. "I am trying to stay alive and raw to the voices that speak to me," he declared after the presentation by Moses Znaimer, president of CITY TV and founder of Much-Music. He then added, in a frequently quoted and quintessential remark, that

If I had been given this attention when I was twenty-six, it would have turned my head. At thirty-six, it might have confirmed my flight on a rather morbid spiritual path. At forty-six, it would have rubbed my nose in my failing powers and have prompted a plotting of a getaway and an alibi. But at fifty-six — hell, I'm just hitting my stride and it doesn't hurt at all. (Qtd. in Pearson 49)

Cohen also won a Juno Award for Songwriter of the Year for "Bird on the Wire."

On 19 April 1991, Cohen was honoured with an even more prestigious award when he was appointed an Officer of the Order of Canada. At his Ottawa investiture on 30 October 1991, he was celebrated in the citation as

one of the most popular and influential writers of his generation whose work has . . . made Canadian literature familiar to readers abroad. Images of beauty, despair, outrage and tenderness are found in his lyrical poetry and prose, whose themes of love, loss and loneliness touch a universal chord in us all.

In that month Cohen was also a surprise guest at a salute to his long-time mentor, Irving Layton, at the International Festival of Authors in Toronto. "Exposure to this work," he told the audience, "moves us. . . . This is the tonic, the elixir. . . . I salute the aching and triumphant impeccability of your life," he concluded (qtd. in "A Salute"). An anthology of forty-three of his songs also appeared that year, to date the largest songbook of Cohen's work.

In April 1992, Cohen gave a *Los Angeles Times* interview in advance of the fall release of his next album, *The Future*, a four-year project originally entitled "Busted." Having moved to Los Angeles in order to spend at least six months each winter near his Zen master and the recording studios (the spring and summer, when not touring, Cohen usually spends in Montreal), he lives in a two-storey duplex, not far from the Jewish district surrounding Fairfax Avenue, that, at the time of *The Future*, he shared with his eighteen-year-old daughter, Lorca. His son, pursuing musical interests, divided his time between Montreal and his mother's apartment in Paris, although more recently he has attended Syracuse University. Cohen has reported that he rarely ventures very far in Los Angeles, not much beyond a favoured Crenshaw-district café. During the 1992 riots, Cohen observed the destruction in south-central Los Angeles, seeing his grocery store, music-supply store, and electronics store all go up in flames. "From my balcony I could see five great fires. The air was thick with cinders." But he had expected this: "having been writing about such things for so long, it was not a surprise," he recently told an English reporter (qtd. in Walsh 40).

Cohen begins most days by visiting a *zendo*, a Zen Buddhist meditation centre, often rising at 4:30 a.m.; he then returns home to compose, deal with business matters, or swim. The house consists of a meditation room on the first floor and a former weight room; upstairs are his sparse quarters, painted and furnished in extreme white, the white of Hydra, with bleached floors. All is austerely furnished, including the bedroom, its only surprises being a black television, portable tape deck, and CD player. Surrounding a mirror in the hall is a collection of caps and hats. A menorah is evident on one of his several wooden tables, as well as the occasional gold candlestick. His workroom off the living room is, by contrast, high-tech, with a synthesizer, fax machine, and Mac Classic computer that he often uses for freehand computer graphics. Here Cohen composes, arranges, and rearranges his music; "Closing Time" on *The Future* demonstrates this process well.

The song began as an up-tempo ballad but in its final form is something of a "demonic" square dance. Cohen has always been an enthusiastic and absorbed arranger, scoring and rescoring material through the difficult process of arranging, the musical equivalent to editing. The unexpected balance between the simplicity of the "Aegean bourgeois" and the complicated world of microchips creates an unusual artisanal atmosphere in the house. In Los Angeles, Cohen is close to musical associates, the recording studios, and, until recently, his companion Rebecca De Mornay, the actress he has been seeing since 1991. He dedicated *The Future* to her and acknowledged her assistance with the selections for *Stranger Music*. Robert Altman introduced them to each other some years ago. In crediting her with conceptualizing the sound on his recent record, Cohen cited a passage from Genesis 24 about virtuous Rebecca drawing water from a well for Abraham's thirsty servant.

The anguish that once characterized much of his work has been replaced by what Cohen more objectively calls "discomfort." But, as he adds, he is reluctant to discuss these matters "because they are essentially . . . of a religious nature, intimately connected to my work. That discomfort is refined in the crucible of attention and intuition and surrender, and what there is to say of it is in the work itself" (qtd. in Teitelbaum 53).

The November 1992 release of *The Future* dispelled all thought that Cohen's popularity had peaked. He planned originally to record the album in Montreal with the team that had produced *I'm Your Man*, but, when he went to Los Angeles to co-opt Warnes as a backup singer for "Democracy," he continued to work there and didn't leave for several years. He finds the city a dangerous but compelling locale: "It's a risky place to live. . . . It's a place that's falling apart. Geologically, the ground is splitting" (qtd. in Walsh 40). Yet, when telephoned in the spring of 1993 to see if he had survived a recent earthquake, he told the caller that he had been at the *zendo* when the tremors struck: "It was beautiful, man. Nobody broke position," he reported (qtd. in Wieseltier 45).

The Future was a hit with *Time*, *Rolling Stone*, *Stereo Review*, and other journals, as well as with the public, although the long tracks reduced its airtime on radio, a particular problem with Cohen's songs. "Democracy," in fact, is over seven minutes long; his campy version of "Always" is over eight. Nonetheless, the album sold more than 100,000 copies in Canada in its first four months, earning platinum status, and spawned an award-winning video for "Closing Time." Interviews appeared everywhere, and Cohen gladly shared with reporters and the public the background and four years of hard work on the album. And through it all, he maintained his cool, autographing a white leather shoe offered to him at the Toronto launch party for the album with his name and the sentence "Magic is afoot" from *Beautiful Losers* (Johnson 63). He frequently explained the genesis of his songs, including the centrepiece, "Democracy," an ironic paean to America; its fourth stanza reads:

It's coming to America first,
the cradle of the best and the worst.
It's here they got the range
and the machinery for change
and it's here they got the spiritual thirst.
It's here the family's broken
and it's here the lonely say
that the heart has got to open

in a fundamental way:
Democracy is coming to the U.S.A.

Marking the song's immediate popularity was its performance by Don Henley at the MTV ball in Washington during the January 1993 inauguration of President Bill Clinton.

Other remarkable songs on the album include a rummy version of Irving Berlin's "Always," recorded in the early hours of the morning in an isolated California studio, and a modern-day "Anthem," borrowing from Kabbalistic sources, especially the sixteenth-century Rabbi Isaac Luria, and expressing a critical idea of hope:

Ring the bells that still can ring.
Forget your perfect offering.
There is a crack in everything.
That's how the light gets in.

The rhythmic "Closing Time," and the pensive "Waiting for the Miracle," balance the essentially pessimistic opening song, "The Future." This political and moral declaration sets a powerful but negative tone for the album, which is quickly undercut by the desire to wait for the miracle, the next song. But the vision is dark, and the ironic wish to return to the totalitarian views of the past is represented by the closing verse, which defines the future in one word: murder.

The blend of despair and hope in the album partly explains its appeal; so, too, does its musicianship. There is a professionalism and maturity in the sound that marks Cohen's eleventh album as a masterful expression of his vision, which is supported by lyrics of substance. Its positive reception initiated another European tour throughout the late spring and summer of 1993: Europe, then New York, Washington, Toronto, Winnipeg, Vancouver, and Victoria, ending in Los Angeles at the Wiltern Theatre on 5 July, although extended bookings in Canada took Cohen back there in late July 1993.

Recognitions continued to accrue: McGill University awarded

FIGURE 20

Cohen in concert with Perla Batalla
and Julie Christensen in 1988.

Cohen an honorary degree on 16 June 1992 (appropriately, Bloomsday, the date of Joyce's *Ulysses*), with Louis Dudek, his former professor and "literary godfather," presenting him to the chancellor for conferral. A November 1992 *New York Times* article praises Cohen as "a singular entity: a kind of rock-and-roll Lord Byron, a cultural scholar in the unlikely medium of pop" (Schoemer). On 21 March 1993, Cohen received the Male Vocalist of the Year Award at the Juno Awards ceremony in Toronto. He also won the award for best video for "Closing Time," set in a Toronto honky-tonk bar, the Matador Club, owned by Cohen's friend Ann Dunn. A recent article on him in the *New Yorker* underscores the Cohen phenomenon, emphasizing his resiliency and persistent appeal to generations of listeners (see Wieseltier), which a writer in *Maclean's* nicely summarizes: "Although he has occasionally faded from the scene, he has never really fallen from fashion" (Johnson 63).

A one-hour CBC Radio show entitled "The Gospel According to Leonard Cohen," broadcast 12 September 1993, highlighted an interview conducted in Montreal, supported by cuts from his best-known songs. The interview surveyed his spiritual views and confirmed his identity as a "minstrel." This broadcast anticipated more public attention with the announcement on 5 October 1993 that Cohen had won a Governor General's Performing Arts Award for his contribution to Canadian music. Formal presentation of the ten-thousand-dollar award was made in Ottawa on 26 November by Governor General Ramon Hnatyshyn, followed by a gala the next evening, at the National Arts Centre, that celebrated the achievements of Cohen and the seven other winners.

The publication in Canada on 13 November 1993 of *Stranger Music: Selected Poems and Songs* marked a plateau in Cohen's writing career. Earlier entitled "New Selected Poems," "If the Moon Has a Sister," and, amusingly, by Adrienne Clarkson — shown assisting Cohen in choosing material (in footage shot in his Montreal home) on her 1989 show "Leonard Cohen" on *Adrienne Clarkson Presents* — as "Everything I'm Not Embarrassed By," the 415-page book is comprised of selections from his formerly out-of-print poetry supplemented by the lyrics to many of his songs. Appearing also in the United States and Great Britain, it is the first of his books dedicated to his children, Adam and Lorca. The poems and songs were chosen by several friends, but Cohen approved the selections and, in some cases, reworked them. Yet they stand as an important, one-volume reminder of the union of poet and songwriter, which have never been separated for him. The recent publication of *Beautiful Losers* in an American paperback has also enlarged his readership. Cohen has commented that "it's very agreeable at 58 to see these books you wrote at 25, 28. I'm delighted. You do have that sense of vindication somehow. You do feel that you're standing in that long tradition of people who were really misunderstood in their time and then re-discovered" (qtd. in Ruhlmann 56).

Virtually coinciding with the publication of *Stranger Music* was the first conference in Canada held exclusively on Cohen and his work, a two-and-a-half-day gathering in Red Deer, Alberta (22–24 October 1993), which drew critics, writers, and musicians, including one of his current backup singers, Perla Batalla. During the time spent debating, criticizing, and admiring Cohen's work, videos and films by and about Cohen played continuously. Papers from the conference appeared in a special issue of *Canadian Poetry* (1993) devoted to him. These and other events underscore the academic as well as public recognition of Cohen, which his fans acknowledged long ago.

In constantly underscoring the need for a spiritual existence in an irreligious time, Cohen marks out a special place of dignity, paralleled by his engagement with the virtually holy act of writing and composing. Hence his posture in the cover photo of *Stranger Music*: his head bent down in contemplation, he sits cross-legged in a Buddhist pose, suggestively suspended over the ground and clearly uninterested in the viewer's gaze. He is spiritually self-absorbed. Only discipline and self-exploration, he has repeated, can supplant his often bone-dry creativity in contrast to other, more productive artists. While it may take Dylan only fifteen minutes to write a song, it takes Cohen years: "You shatter versions of the self until you get down to a line, a word, that you can defend, that you can wrap your voice around without choking," he declared (qtd. in Johnson 66).

"My Life in Art" is a deliberately chosen title for the statements in *Death of a Lady's Man*. Yet with this awareness of the commitment to poetry and song comes the humbleness (successor to the victimization) that also defines Cohen's work and performances. Before the power of the voice and the word — and what they can convey — Cohen stands with bowed head and gratitude because he understands the responsibility of creation and the integrity required to make a work honest. Judaism, Yoga, Buddhism, fasting, vegetarianism, love, drugs, poetry, song, painting — all are steps in his search for the freedom of simplicity. But Cohen also knows that not everyone can experience this freedom; consequently, he constantly offers thanks to those who attempt to comprehend him as he attempts to break down the barriers between listener and performer, stage and audience — as he tries to stand aside from the words and to let their power speak, thereby allowing the newsreel to become the feature, as he writes in *Beautiful Losers*. In the first phase of his career, life and its ritual symbols formed his art, providing the substance for, and shape of, his writing; in the second, art, as symbolic and religious expression, has fashioned his life.

Once asked if he liked himself, Cohen replied — after a pause — that he liked only his "true self," which he has constantly sought to discover (qtd. in Saltzman 80). Through his art, spiritual journeys, romantic relationships, and retreats, he continues to define himself. But the feelings that he studies, he masters, thus providing an integrity for all that he undertakes. He remains a figure of spirit, decorum, and intensity, managing to make sadness into a career, say the ungenerous, and to elevate despair to understanding, say his admirers. Art, united with the recognition of the necessity of spirit in a world inhospitable to its presence, has been the means for Leonard Cohen to join the coordinates of his life.

FIGURE 21

At the Matador Club, Toronto, in 1993.

CHRONOLOGY

1887   Nathaniel Bernard Cohen, Cohen's father, born.

1907   Masha Klinitsky-Klein, Cohen's mother, born.

1930   Esther Cohen, Cohen's sister, born.

1934   Leonard Norman Cohen born in Montreal on 21 September.

1936   Federico Garciá Lorca assassinated by anti-Republican fascist rebels in Granada in August, possibly on the 18th, at the beginning of the Spanish Civil War.

1944   Cohen's father dies.

1949   Cohen reads Lorca's poetry for the first time and briefly meets Irving Layton.

1950   Cohen begins writing poetry in the summer.

1951   He begins attending McGill University on 21 September. Over his four-year university career, he will have Hugh MacLennan, F.R. Scott, and Louis Dudek as professors.

1953   Cohen's first poem, "An Halloween Poem to Delight My Younger Friends," published in *CIV/n*, the new poetry journal edited by Aileen Collins. Dudek and Layton are editorial advisors.

1954   Cohen renews his acquaintance with Layton, and their forty-year friendship begins.

1955   Cohen graduates from McGill, winning the MacNaughton Prize for creative writing. He and Layton attend the Canadian Writers' Conference at Queen's University, 28–31 July.

1956   *Let Us Compare Mythologies* published as the first title in the McGill Poetry Series, edited by Dudek. Cohen records eight poems from the book for the Folkways album, *Six Montreal Poets*, released in 1957. Included on the record are A.J.M. Smith, Layton, Dudek, Scott, and A.M. Klein.

1956–57 Cohen attends Columbia University, enrolled in the General Studies Program. In April he edits the *Phoenix* at Columbia, and in July he completes a draft of his unpublished novel "A Ballet of Lepers."

1958 Cohen attempts a short-lived career in the clothing industry. He is a counsellor at Pripstein's Summer Camp.

1959 He wins a two-thousand-dollar Canada Council Arts Scholarship in April. He departs for England in November and leaves London for Greece in December, settling on Hydra in March 1960.

1960 Cohen returns to Montreal in November and begins collaborative playwriting with Layton.

1961 Cohen visits Cuba in April, wins a one-thousand-dollar Canada Council Arts Scholarship, has *The Spice-Box of Earth* published, and returns to Hydra in August.

1963 *The Favorite Game* published in England and the United States.

1964 *Flowers for Hitler* published. Cohen wins a Quebec literary prize for *The Favorite Game*.

1965 *Ladies and Gentlemen . . . Mr. Leonard Cohen*, a National Film Board documentary directed by Donald Brittain and Don Owen, released.

1966 *Beautiful Losers* and *Parasites of Heaven* published. In late spring Cohen arrives in New York on his way to Nashville; he joins the folk-rock scene and records his first album after being signed to Columbia by John Hammond. Judy Collins releases *In My Life* with Cohen's "Suzanne."

1967 In April Cohen has his first concert appearance, at Town Hall in New York City. Judy Collins releases *Wild Flowers* with three songs by Cohen.

1968 *Songs of Leonard Cohen*, his first album, released. *Selected Poems 1956–1968* published. Cohen meets Joshu Sasaki Roshi, a Zen master, and their twenty-six-year friendship begins.

1969	Cohen declines the 1968 Governor General's Literary Award for English-language poetry for *Selected Poems 1956–1968*. *Songs from a Room* released in April.
1970	Cohen has his first European concert tour, consisting of seven shows, in May. In May he also receives an honorary degree from Dalhousie University.
1971	*Songs of Love and Hate* released in March. *McCabe and Mrs. Miller*, a film by Robert Altman, released with a soundtrack by Cohen.
1972	*The Energy of Slaves* published.
1973	*Live Songs* released in April. Cohen travels to Israel in October to begin a two-month tour of duty during the Yom Kippur War and its aftermath.
1974	*New Skin for the Old Ceremony* released in August.
1975	*The Best of Leonard Cohen* released in November.
1977	*Death of a Ladies' Man*, the album, released.
1978	Cohen's mother dies.
1979	*Recent Songs* released in September.
1984	*Book of Mercy* published.
1985	*Various Positions* released in February.
1986	*Famous Blue Raincoat*, by Jennifer Warnes, released.
1988	*I'm Your Man* released in February.
1991	*I'm Your Fan*, a tribute album, released. Cohen inducted into the Juno Hall of Fame on 3 March. On 19 April he is appointed to the Order of Canada; the investiture by the Governor General occurs on 30 October.
1992	Cohen receives an honorary degree from McGill University in June. *The Future* released in November.
1993	On 21 March Cohen receives a Juno Award for Male Vocalist of the Year; "Closing Time" wins the Juno Award for Best Video. In October Cohen wins the Governor General's Performing Arts Award, which he receives in Ottawa on 26 November; he is celebrated the next day in a gala performance at the National Arts Centre. *Stranger Music: Selected Poems and Songs* published in November in Canada, the United States, and Great Britain.

DISCOGRAPHY

Songs of Leonard Cohen. Columbia, CL 2733, 1968.

SIDE ONE:
Suzanne
Master Song
Winter Lady
The Stranger Song
Sisters of Mercy

SIDE TWO:
So Long, Marianne
Hey, That's No Way to Say Goodbye
Stories of the Street
Teachers
One of Us Cannot Be Wrong

Songs from a Room. Columbia, CS 9767, 1969.

SIDE ONE:
Bird on the Wire
Story of Isaac
A Bunch of Lonesome Heroes
The Partisan
Seems So Long Ago, Nancy

SIDE TWO:
The Old Revolution
The Butcher
You Know Who I Am
Lady Midnight
Tonight Will Be Fine

Songs of Love and Hate. Columbia, C 30103, 1971.

SIDE ONE:
Love Calls You by Your Name
Dress Rehearsal Rag
Avalanche
Last Year's Man

SIDE TWO:
Diamonds in the Mine
Sing Another Song, Boys
Joan of Arc
Famous Blue Raincoat

Live Songs. Columbia, KC 31724, 1973.

SIDE ONE:
Minute Prologue
Passing Thru
You Know Who I Am
Bird on the Wire
Nancy
Improvisation

SIDE TWO:
Story of Isaac
Please Don't Pass Me By
Tonight Will Be Fine
Queen Victoria

New Skin for the Old Ceremony. Columbia, KC 33167, 1974.

SIDE ONE:
Is This What You Wanted
Chelsea Hotel #2
Lover Lover Lover
Field Commander Cohen
Why Don't You Try

SIDE TWO:
There Is a War
A Singer Must Die
I Tried to Leave You
Who by Fire
Take This Longing
Leaving Greensleeves

The Best of Leonard Cohen. Columbia, WES 90334, 1975.

SIDE ONE:
Suzanne
Sisters of Mercy
So Long, Marianne
Lady Midnight
The Partisan
Bird on the Wire

SIDE TWO:
Hey, That's No Way to Say Goodbye
Famous Blue Raincoat
Last Year's Man
Chelsea Hotel #2
Who by Fire
Take This Longing

Death of a Ladies' Man. Columbia, 90436, 1977.

SIDE ONE:
True Love Leaves No Traces
Iodine
Paper-Thin Hotel
Memories

SIDE TWO:
I Left a Woman Waiting
Don't Go Home with Your Hard-On
Fingerprints
Death of a Ladies' Man

Recent Songs. Columbia, KC 36364, 1979.

SIDE ONE:
The Guests
Humbled in Love
The Window
Came So Far for Beauty
The Lost Canadian

SIDE TWO:
The Traitor
Our Land of Solitude
The Gypsy's Wife
The Smokey Life
Ballad of the Absent Mare

Various Positions. Passport, PCC 90728, 1985.

SIDE ONE:
Dance Me to the End of Love
Coming Back to You
The Law
Night Comes On
Hallelujah

SIDE TWO:
The Captain
Hunter's Lullaby
Heart with No Companion
If It Be Your Will

I'm Your Man. Columbia, FC 44191, 1988.

SIDE ONE:
First We Take Manhattan
Ain't No Cure for Love
Everybody Knows
I'm Your Man
Take This Waltz

SIDE TWO:
Jazz Police
I Can't Forget
Tower of Song

The Future. Columbia-Sony, CK 53226, 1992.

SIDE ONE:
The Future
Waiting for the Miracle
Be for Real
Closing Time
Anthem

SIDE TWO:
Democracy
Light as the Breeze
Always
Tacoma Trailer

Cohen also appears as a guest artist on Earl Scrugg's *Anniversary Special* (Columbia, KC 33416) and on Jennifer Warnes's *Famous Blue Raincoat* (Attic, 1227). Among his singles, which first appeared in March 1968 with the release of *Suzanne/So Long, Marianne* (CBS, 3337), are *Bird on the Wire* (live)/*Tonight Will Be Fine* (live) (CBS, 2494, 1974), *First We Take Manhattan/Sisters of Mercy* (CBS, 65 1352–7, 1988), and the more recent *Democracy Is Coming to the USA* (Columbia, 44K 74778, 1992), which includes "Democracy" from *The Future* plus "First We Take Manhattan" and "I'm Your Man" from *I'm Your Man*.

The 1991 tribute album, *I'm Your Fan*, produced by Christian Fevret and Jean-Daniel Beauvallet for *Les inrockuptibles* and released by Warner Music (17 55984 CR), contains the following songs and performers:

SIDE ONE

Who by Fire
  The House of Love
Hey, That's No Way to Say Goodbye
  Ian McCulloch
I Can't Forget
  The Pixies
Stories of the Street
  That Petrol Emotion
Bird on the Wire
  The Lilac Time

Suzanne
  Geoffrey Oryema
So Long, Marianne
  James
Avalanche IV
  Jean-Louis Murat
Don't Go Home with Your Hard-On
  David McComb and Adam Peters

SIDE TWO:

First We Take Manhattan
  REM
Chelsea Hotel #2
  Lloyd Cole
Tower of Song
  Robert Forster
Tower of Song
  Nick Cave and the Bad Seeds
Take This Longing
  Peter Astor
True Love Leaves No Traces
  Dead Famous People
I'm Your Man
  Bill Pritchard
A Singer Must Die
  Fatima Mansions
Hallelujah
  John Cale

WORKS CONSULTED

Advertisement. *New York Times* 29 Sept. 1968, sec. 7: 21.

Altman, Robert. "Robert Altman Is Back in the Spotlight: But . . . He's Still Been Quite Busy during the Last Decade." With Dan McLeod. *Georgia Straight* 8–15 Oct. 1993: 15.

Ballantyne, Michael. "Poet-Novelist Reflects on the Quebec Scene." *Entertainments* [supp. to *Montreal Star*] 26 Oct. 1963: 2–3.

Batten, Jack. "Tears and Triumphs in Pop's Passing Parade — and Awards to Match." *Globe and Mail* [Toronto] 25 Dec. 1970: 29.

Beissel, Henry, and Joy Bennett, eds. *Raging Like a Fire: A Celebration of Irving Layton.* Montreal: Véhicule, 1993.

bissett, bill. "! ! ! ! !" Rev. of *Beautiful Losers. Alphabet* 13 (1967): 94–95.

Browne, David. "7 Reasons Leonard Cohen Is the Next-Best Thing to God: Or, Why an Aging Beatnik Is Adored by Cutting-Edge Rockers." *Entertainment Weekly* 8 Jan. 1993: 26+.

Cameron, Elspeth. *Hugh MacLennan: A Writer's Life.* Toronto: U of Toronto P, 1981.

——. *Irving Layton: A Portrait.* Toronto: Stoddart, 1985.

Cocks, Jay. "Getting On a New Train." Rev. of *The Future. Time* [Can. ed.] 25 Jan. 1993: 57.

Cohen, Leonard. "After the Wipe-Out, a Renewal." With Sandra Djwa. *Ubyssey* [U of British Columbia] 3 Feb. 1967: 8.

——. *Beautiful Losers.* New York: Viking, 1966.

——. *The Best of Leonard Cohen.* Columbia, WES 90334, 1975.

——. *Book of Mercy.* Toronto: McClelland, 1984.

——. "Comme un guerrier: An Interview with Leonard Cohen." With Christian Fevret. Trans. Sophie Miller. *Throat Culture* 3 (1992): 20+.

——. *Death of a Ladies' Man.* Columbia, 90436, 1977.

——. *Death of a Lady's Man.* Toronto: McClelland, 1978.

——. *The Energy of Slaves.* Toronto: McClelland, 1972.

———. *The Favorite Game*. New York: Viking, 1963.

———. *The Favourite Game*. New Canadian Library 73. Toronto: McClelland, 1970.

———. *Flowers for Hitler*. Toronto: McClelland, 1964.

———. *The Future*. Columbia-Sony, CK 53226, 1992.

———. *I'm Your Man*. Columbia, FC 44191, 1988.

———. "Leonard Cohen." With Alan Twigg. *Strong Voices: Conversations with Fifty Canadian Authors*. Ed. Twigg. Madeira Park, BC: Harbour, 1988. 41–47.

———. "Leonard Cohen." With Doug Fetherling. *Books in Canada* Aug.–Sept. 1984: 29–30.

———. "Leonard Cohen." With Peter Gzowski. *Morningside*. CBC Radio. 18 Nov. 1992.

———. *Leonard Cohen Anthology*. New York: Amsco, 1991. [Lyric sheets for 43 songs.]

———. "Leonard Cohen: The Poet as Hero: 2." With Michael Harris. *Saturday Night* June 1969: 26–31.

———. *Let Us Compare Mythologies*. Illus. Freda Guttman. McGill Poetry Series 1. Toronto: Contact, 1956.

———. *Live Songs*. Columbia, KC 31724, [1973].

———. "Loneliness and History." Manuscript Collection 122. Thomas Fisher Rare Book Library, U of Toronto, Toronto.

———. *New Skin for the Old Ceremony*. Columbia, KC 33167, 1974.

———. *Parasites of Heaven*. Toronto: McClelland, 1966.

———. *Recent Songs*. Columbia, KC 36364, 1979.

———. *Selected Poems 1956–1968*. Toronto: McClelland, 1968.

———. "Sincerely, L. Cohen: Twenty-Five Years after 'Suzanne' Made Him a Hippie Icon, Leonard Cohen May Be the Finest Songwriter in America." With Brian Cullman. *Details* Jan. 1993: 101+.

———, et al. *Six Montreal Poets*. Folkways, FL 9805, 1957.

———. *Songs from a Room*. Columbia, CS 9767, [1969].

———. *Songs of Leonard Cohen*. Columbia, CL 2733, [1968].

———. *Songs of Leonard Cohen*. Ed. Harvey Vinson. New York: Amsco, 1969. [Lyric sheets for 20 songs.]

———. *Songs of Love and Hate*. Columbia, C 30103, [1971].

———. *Songs of Love and Hate*. New York: Amsco, 1972. [Arrangements for voice and guitar.]

———. *The Spice-Box of Earth*. Toronto: McClelland, 1961.

——. *Stranger Music: Selected Poems and Songs.* Toronto: McClelland, 1993.

——. *Various Positions.* Passport, PCC 90728, 1985.

"Cohen, Leonard." *The Penguin Encyclopedia of Popular Music.* 1989.

Collins, Judy. *Trust Your Heart: An Autobiography.* Boston: Houghton, 1987.

Dorman, Loranne S., and Clive L. Rawlins. *Leonard Cohen: Prophet of the Heart.* London, Eng.: Omnibus, 1990.

Djwa, Sandra. *The Politics of the Imagination: A Life of F.R. Scott.* Toronto: McClelland, 1987.

Dudek, Louis, ed. *Poetry of Our Time: An Introduction to Twentieth-Century Poetry Including Modern Canadian Poetry.* Toronto: Macmillan, 1966.

Dudek, Louis, Irving Layton, and Raymond Souster. *Cerberus.* Toronto: Contact, 1952.

Dudek, Louis. Letter to the author. 20 July 1993.

Faulkner, William. "The Bear." *The Portable Faulkner.* Rev. ed. Ed. Malcolm Cowley. Harmondsworth, Eng.: Penguin, 1977. 197–320.

Fetherling, Douglas. *Some Day Soon: Essays on Canadian Songwriters.* Kingston: Quarry, 1991.

Fodor's Modern Guides: Greece. Ed. Eugene Fodor and William Curtis. London, Eng.: MacGibbon, 1963.

Gnarowski, Michael, ed. *Leonard Cohen: The Artist and His Critics.* Critical Views on Canadian Writers. Toronto: McGraw, 1976.

Godfrey, Stephen. "A New Artistic Twist for Pied Piper Poet." *Globe and Mail* [Toronto] 1 Mar. 1980: E1.

Goldstein, Richard. "Beautiful Creep." *Village Voice* 28 Dec. 1967: 18+. Rpt. in Gnarowski 40–45.

"The Gospel According to Leonard Cohen." CBC Radio. 12 Sept. 1993.

Gustafson, Ralph. "Homage to Irving Layton." Beissel and Bennett 95–99.

Hutcheon, Linda. "Leonard Cohen (1934–)." *Canadian Writers and Their Works.* Fiction Series. Ed. Robert Lecker, Jack David, and Ellen Quigley. Vol. 10. Toronto: ECW, 1989. 25–65. 10 vols. to date. 1981– .

——. "Leonard Cohen (1934–)." *Canadian Writers and Their Works.* Poetry Series. Ed. Robert Lecker, Jack David, and Ellen Quigley. Vol. 10. Toronto: ECW, 1992. 21–65. 10 vols. to date. 1981– .

Jackson, Alan. "Growing Old Passionately." *Observer* [London, Eng.] 22 Nov. 1992: ARTS 3/59.

Johnson, Brian D. "Life of a Lady's Man: Leonard Cohen Sings of Love and Freedom." *Maclean's* 7 Dec. 1992: 63+.

Kapica, Jack. "The Trials of Leonard Cohen." *Gazette* [Montreal] 25 Aug. 1973: 37.

Kaye, Leslie L., ed. *The McGill Chapbook*. Toronto: Ryerson, 1959.

Klein, A.M. *The Collected Poems of A.M. Klein*. Ed. Miriam Waddington. Toronto: McGraw, 1974.

Ladies and Gentlemen . . . Mr. Leonard Cohen. Dir. Donald Brittain and Don Owen. NFB, 1965.

Layton, Irving. *Balls for a One-Armed Juggler*. Toronto: McClelland, 1963.

——. "An Interview with Irving Layton." *Canadian Theatre Review* 14 (1977): 54–55.

——. Letter to Desmond Pacey. 28 Aug. 1961.

"Leonard Cohen." *Adrienne Clarkson Presents*. CBC Television. 1989.

"Leonard Cohen." Sony Music Biography. Sony, 1992.

Lorca, Federico García. *Collected Poems*. Ed. Christopher Maurer. Trans. Francisco Aragon et al. New York: Farrar, 1991. Vol. 2 of *The Poetical Works of Federico García Lorca*. Ed. Maurer. 2 vols. 1988–91.

——. *Poet in New York*. Ed. Christopher Maurer. Trans. Greg Simon and Steven F. White. New York: Farrar, 1988. Vol. 1 of *The Poetical Works of Federico García Lorca*. Ed. Maurer. 2 vols. 1988–91.

Lumsden, Susan. "Leonard Cohen Wants the 'Unconditional Leadership of the World.' " *Weekend Magazine* 12 Sept. 1970: 22–25. Rpt. in Gnarowski 69–73.

Lyons, Roberta. "Jewish Poets from Montreal: Concepts of History in the Poetry of A.M. Klein, Irving Layton, and Leonard Cohen." MA thesis Carleton U, 1966.

MacLennan, Hugh. *Two Solitudes*. Toronto: Collins, 1945.

MacSkimming, Roy. "The Importance of Knowing Irving: A Memoir, in Lieu of a Biography." Beissel and Bennett 11–19.

——. " 'New' Leonard Cohen Opens Up His Thoughts." *Toronto Star* 22 Jan. 1975: E16.

Mandel, Eli. "Cohen's Life as a Slave." *Another Time*. By Mandel. Three Solitudes: Contemporary Literary Criticism in Canada 3.

Erin, ON: Porcépic, 1977. 124–36.

——. "Leonard Cohen's Brilliant Con Game." Rev. of *Death of a Lady's Man. Saturday Night* Nov. 1978: 51–53.

McCann, Wendy. "Return to Canada Pays Off for Dion, Cohen and Others." *Vancouver Sun* 22 Mar. 1993: C1.

Murphy, Karen, and Ronald Gross. " 'All You Need Is Love. Love Is All You Need.' So Writes a Rock Poet. But Is That Poetry?" *New York Times Magazine* 13 Apr. 1969: 36+.

Ondaatje, Michael. *Leonard Cohen.* Canadian Writers 5. New Canadian Library. Toronto: McClelland, 1970.

Owen, Don. "Leonard Cohen: The Poet as Hero: 3." *Saturday Night* June 1969: 31–32.

Pearson, Ian. "Growing Old Disgracefully: Leonard Cohen . . . Has Transformed Himself into . . . One of the Best Songwriters Around." *Saturday Night* Mar. 1993: 44+.

"Poets' Progress." *Time* [Can. ed.] 6 Nov. 1964: 16.

Poore, Charles. "Young Bohemians — Canadian Style." Rev. of *The Favorite Game. New York Times* 12 Sept. 1963: 35.

Press release. New York: Viking, 1963.

Purdy, A.W. "Leonard Cohen: A Personal Look." *Canadian Literature* 23 (1965): 7–16.

Ruddy, Jon. "Is the World (or Anybody) Ready for Leonard Cohen?" *Maclean's* 1 Oct. 1966: 18+.

Ruhlmann, William. "The Stranger Music of Leonard Cohen." *Goldmine* 19 Feb. 1993: 10+.

Saltzman, Paul. "Famous Last Words from Leonard Cohen." *Maclean's* June 1972: 6+.

"A Salute to Layton." *Globe and Mail* [Toronto] 25 Oct. 1991: C6.

Schoemer, Karen. "Leonard Cohen, the Lord Byron of Rock-and-Roll." *New York Times* 29 Nov. 1992, sec. 2: 24.

Scobie, Stephen. *Leonard Cohen.* Vancouver: Douglas, 1978.

Sharp, Ken. "Porridge? Lozenge? Syringe?" *Q* [London, Eng.] 1991: 77–82.

Sloman, Larry. *On the Road with Bob Dylan: Rolling with the Thunder.* New York: Bantam, 1978.

Stone, Jay. "Introducing Leonard Cohen, Family Man: From the 'Ashes' of His Poetry, a Father Figure Emerges." *Ottawa Citizen* 28 Nov. 1993: B5.

Teitelbaum, Sheldon. "Leonard Cohen, Pain Free." *Los Angeles Times Magazine* 5 Apr. 1992: 22+.

Trocchi, Alexander. *Cain's Book*. New York: Grove, 1960.

Walsh, John. "Melancholy Baby." *Independent Magazine* [London, Eng.] 8 May 1993: 38–40.

Whiteman, Bruce. "Leonard Cohen: An Annotated Bibliography." *The Annotated Bibliography of Canada's Major Authors*. Ed. Robert Lecker and Jack David. Vol. 2. Downsview, ON: ECW, 1980. 55–95. 8 vols. to date. 1979– .

Wieseltier, Leon. "The Prince of Bummers: Leonard Cohen's Songs . . . May Be Fascinated by the Fallen, but He Has Ways of Rising above It All." *New Yorker* 26 July 1993: 40–45.

Williams, Stephen. "The Confessions of Leonard Cohen." *Toronto Life* Feb. 1978: 48+.

Wilson, Milton. Rev. of *Flowers for Hitler* [part of "Poetry" sec. of "Letters in Canada: 1964"]. *University of Toronto Quarterly* 34.4 (1965): 352–54. Rpt. in Gnarowski 20–22.